COSMIC BIBLE

Paradigm Revolution
by Paradoxical Truth

BOOK 1

Minoru Uba

Copyright © 2015 by Minoru Uba

COSMIC BIBLE

Published by Babel Press U.S.A.
All rights reserved.
Date of publication: April 3, 2015

This book was originally published in Japanese under the title "宇宙聖書" by VOICE, Japan in 2010.

Author: Minoru Uba

Director: Tomoki Hotta

Original translation by Self-Healing Study and Practice Group
Edited and translated by Gyoko Koike

Coordinator: Junko Rodriguez
Formatting: Sota Torigoe

ISBN: 978-0989232623

Babel Corporation
Pacific Business News Bldg. #208,
1833 Kalakaua Avenue,
Honolulu, Hawaii 96815

Phone: (808) 946 - 3773
Fax: (808) 946 - 3993

Website: http://www.bookandright.com/

CONTENTS

Preface by Minoru Uba………6

Chapter One ☆ The Starting Point

1-1. Stress induced by self-injurious behavior…..12

1-2. The difference between remission and cure…..18

1-3. Dimensional integration from individual purpose to entire purpose…..20

1-4. The nature and individuality choose a path to health or disease…..23

1-5. "Surprising Phenomenon" and the effect of drugs…..25

1-6. Boundaries between medicine and risk…..32

1-7. Common existing purpose and value of life…..32

1-8. Cells complete the individual purpose for the entire purpose…..35

1-9. Scientific reason and fluctuations of relativity…..37

1-10. PAREVO and the world of individuality wave…..39

1-11. PAREVO makes bloom, endless creativity power…..41

1-12. The way of life of PAREVO establishes Self-evaluation…..43

1-13. Limitations of the paradigm of the theory of "right and wrong"…..44

1-14. Views of life and death by Self-determination based on the principle of freedom…..50

1-15. Harsh environment shows the way of spiritual evolution…..53

1-16. Up through the 20th century was the era of the "one way method"…..55

1-17. Mass media is the child of the "one-way method"…..57
1-18. The 21st century is the interactive era…..59
1-19. Internal threats and the advent of crisis…..62
1-20. Is cancer physical predisposition or mental disposition? …..66
1-21. Threat of mental self-poisoning…..67
1-22. Establishment of the true view of life and death…..69
1-23. Mechanism for mutation in cancer cells…..70
1-24. Self-injurious behavior caused by Self-hatred is the root of all evil…..72
1-25. Crucial differences between cancer cells and normal cells…..74
1-26. The "principles of dimensional domination" based on the rule of "body is subjective and spirit is objective"…..82
1-27. The "principles of dimensional integration" based on the rule of "spirit is subjective and body is objective"…..85
1-28. Individual and whole are based on the "chain of responsibility system"…..87
1-29. Sickness is the "phenomenon of love confirmation"…..90
1-30. Sickness is Self-injurious behavior caused by Self-hatred…..92
1-31. All things are based on the principles of Self-determination and Self-responsibility…..95
1-32. The rule of "exclusion theory by jealousy"…..99
1-33. End of material civilization…..102
1-34. The 21st century is the era of consciousness revolution…..104

Preface

In recent years, our surrounding environments have been changing, such as environmental destruction by global warming, time saving and overload of information brought about by IT-revolution, etc. The world is heading toward the expansion of a disparate society due to degradation of the function of capitalism, self-reliance by sloughing off the dependent structure, and human and cultural exchanges called globalization, so the structure of society has been changing rapidly.

On the other hand, we are still struggling with economic supremacy, academic supremacy, and the science almighty principal that increase the principles of evil competition, which makes winners and losers. On a global scale, there are acts of terrorism, destruction, and actual wars based on religious struggles, fighting for natural resources, and economic supremacy. I think more people are facing the complex stress around their nature, family, and social environments because they cannot keep up with those rapid changes, and feel something is really wrong.

People today are very different from those who lived before the 20th century. We are beginning to realize that true richness is not in economic values but someplace else. Especially young people are beginning to look more for the true purpose of life and the meaning of our existence.

We human beings have wished for immortality since the beginning of our history, trying to live as long as we can. However, we are not able to live forever, so we have to accept death as our fate. More people are realizing the emptiness of living without purpose and meaning, and are now seriously considering how to live for Self-accomplishment for the best death, rather than seeking the ideal life. In other words we must establish the true view of life and death, rather than living life just for living. So, the concept about the way to die has become more important.

Now, the archaic frameworks of religious theories and values, thought and economic frameworks and values, common sense and good judgment on the earth level, based on the "Earth logical evidence" theory will fade away, globally, by the opposite rules and principles which are based on the "Cosmological evidence." The universal principles exist beyond those archaic paradigms and established theories, and consist of the totally opposite rules and principles from those of the star of the earth. I named this revolution with the cosmological framework and values, the Paradigm Revolution, and call it "PARAREVO", by taking the first four letters from each of the two words.

In this book, I verify the history and several phenomena on the earth paradoxically by the universal principles. The rules of the universe are not theories from human beings, for human beings, and by human beings, who are living on the earth. Thus, I decided the title of this book to be "COSMIC BIBLE," implying this is the cosmological BIBLE. "The Earth Bible," in the category of religious theory based on the earth logical evidence, Judaism, Christianity, Islam, Buddhism, and Hinduism, are not able to reach the universal principles, but this "Cosmic Bible" will complete the universal

Preface

principles in each truth of yourself.

The original Japanese book is one book with four chapters; Chapter One☆The Starting Point (introduction), Chapter Two☆The Deriving point (development), Chapter Three☆The Turning point, and Chapter Four☆Conclusion. For English translation, I divided the original book into four separate books making it easier to read. So, BOOK 1 is chapter one, BOOK 2 is chapter two, BOOK 3 is chapter three, and BOOK 4 is chapter four: Conclusion.

In BOOK 1, I mainly explain the way of thinking by PARAREVO toward social phenomena and illness, and several basic concepts of PARAPREVO. In BOOK 2, I analyze consciousnesses, and mention some core concepts of PARAREVO, such as the "triangle relationship of sorrow and ONSHU," by referring to some characters in the Old Testament. In BOOK 3, I explain the mechanism of the universe, and other core concepts of PARAREVO such as the "relative universal original power," the "rule of entropy relativity" and SHINSEI, deeper and how to release important ONSHU relationships such as parent and a child, and husband and wife. In BOOK 4, I summarize the purpose of the life which is to graduate from the earth star by completing the love pair system, and ultimate PARAREVO theory for eternal love and freedom.

Throughout the four BOOKS, I have repeated rules and principals of the universe many times, deliberately. This is because we have been trained by our instinctive survival consciousnesses on the earth star, throughout 3.8 billion years, so I would like to change those habits of mind, and memories which remain imbedded deep inside our DNA. Since many concepts are not easy to explain with existing words, I had to express those with many of my own words, which I have highlighted with quotation marks.

At first, as long as you are dominated by the physical world benefits and undifferentiated sexual desire, and are in a lower spiritual dimension, even if you are highly educated, have a very high IQ, a lot of knowledge about religions, thoughts, and society, or high status and have lots of experiences, you might feel it is difficult to understand the concept of this book. However, if you are a highly spiritual person, in a high spiritual and personality dimension, and have a high EQ and rich and modest mind, you will be able to understand this book easily.

Because our society is so settled in the principal of economic supremacy, it may be hard for you to understand what I want to say in this book. However, I have confidence that when we face the confusion and chaos because of the increasing entropy of society (escalation of disorder) on a global scale, this book will show you the true value. When you read this book with wisdom from your soul, based on the cosmological theory, not based on the earth logical theory and knowledge in the brain, you can understand easily and make a clear distinction between truth and fact, and live the way of PARAREVO, achieving Self-completion with gratitude and happiness.

Cosmic Bible is not the book to satisfy your intelligence and reason, but is "the sacred revelation from the universe" that gives

Preface

you spiritual wisdom and spiritual mind. Especially, there is a lot of content long-awaited for by women, to release their sorrow and ONSHU. When you finish reading, you will find the way to be your real self. I am sure that you will find the real existing purpose and value of why you were born to this earth star, and find your real role and responsibility, on this planet, for Self-completion of your life.

Minoru Uba

Chapter 1

The Starting Point

(Introduction)

Chapter 1 ☆ The Starting Point

1-1. Stress induced by self-injurious behavior

There have appeared various remarkable environmental disasters caused by exhaustion of natural resources, producing more food for consumption, and adding pollutants to the earth, air, and water, which are bringing on global warming and the extinction of thousands of species every year. Because of human egoism, both the economic supreme principle and the science almighty principle reign. Other problems of the modern era have been discovered as well, including the emergence of various toxins such as dioxin (an artificially produced industrial byproduct,) used in farming, and it has become increasingly clear that they have dangerous effects to the human body.

Because of the corruption of sexual morals, intractable diseases such as HIV are now prevalent all over the world. Those are difficult to deal with by religion, politics, and medical science. Also, every year, the mortality rate by cancer is increasing while other new viruses emerge. We human beings are facing a crisis which might reshape the ecosystem of the entire earth.

If we continue our pattern of mass production and mass consumption, following the current theoretical framework and values we presently adhere to, an ethical breakdown will spread on a global scale. Consequently, the global environment and the world order will collapse, and then, we human beings will eventually end up on a path of Self-destruction.

It is necessary to confront these issues, including the corruption of sexual morals, the disintegration of the family unit, ethical breakdown, disorder in the classroom, and the ecological problems caused by the disruption in the natural environment. However, when I consider why those problems have occurred, some simultaneously, some sequentially, I find it difficult to solve them easily, and end up concluding that the problems are created by our current society situation causing stress, induced by *Self-injurious behavior* which is due to the egoism that continued through the 20th century.

We are still constricted by the main governing principles of the 20th century type of power struggle, such as the definition of success, the framework of social theories, values, and science technologies, which are based on the principle of competition.

We must realize the limitations in attempting to create a future global order using the archaic framework of religious theories and values, common sense, and good judgment, all based on the "earth logical evidence" theory (the purpose and the value of the earth level dimension).

When we face these realities, there are two options from which we can choose.

One, we just continue to follow the present framework of social theory and values based on the "earth logical evidence" employed in the 20th century, so that we only strengthen the paradigm as it is. In this way, we will have to face the final crisis with many sacrifices, and then at last, we will be forced to reform the society.

Or the other way, we could change the framework of social theory and values, drastically, to a paradigm based on the "cosmological

Chapter 1 ☆ The Starting Point

evidence" (the existing purpose and the existing value of the universe) and create a crisis free society.

Until February 3, 2010, which according to the PARAREVO theory, was the beginning of women's integration era, with our totally groundless assumption that we were secure in our society, and thinking that the final crisis was far away, we had not radically changed the present theory and framework of the society and values, and followed them without any doubt as to the retention of old fashioned ideas based on the "earth logical evidence." This ignorant fact is allowing us to continue making and taking excessive physical world benefits, such as social status, reputation, property, etc., and any conduct necessary, to seek those desires.

Many measures, reformations and movements, such as poverty, pollution, aging, and environmental measures, medical treatment, welfare, and pension reformations, and peace movements by NGO and NPO, were ultimately legalized by large and powerful organizations with vested interests and were utilized for their excessive physical world benefits.

Actually, they have only functioned as the hotbed for the systematized dishonest politicians and bureaucratic domination in order to maintain the framework of theory and values for the pyramidal society based on the male dominated structure up through the 20th century. Now we are trying to pull ourselves out from all kinds of *inherited negative stress* against social contradictions.

We are also realizing that we must face new world wide crises, such as nuclear terrorism using weapons of mass destruction, which are becoming more and more definitive. Therefore, we must recreate, on a world scale, a new theoretical framework beyond religious theories, based on the "cosmological evidence," and each of us has to complete the paradigm revolution and accomplish the *digital revolution of consciousness*, to create a society without any crisis. Even though it seems very hard, we must choose this way in order to survive, because the perfect collaboration (completed symbiosis), which is the path to Self-enlightenment (transition from the physical to the spiritual vision) and spiritual evolution, can only exist in a new, crisis free society.

I believe that everybody wishes to obtain the true healthy life, which is the completion of a day by *accepting it as it is, unconditionally and totally, with gratitude and happiness*, without discontent, dissatisfaction, deficiency, ONSHU (fluctuation of reason and mental conflict between "soul mind" and "body mind") which everybody has in the soul, or sorrow, caused by unpleasant memories from the past and carrying them forward to the present, and without bringing in anxiety, uneasiness and fear for the future.

Unconditional acceptance means not making criticism and evaluation of good or bad, or superiority or inferiority, toward the outside, but to look inside, separate your "soul mind" (intention which love of the soul directs) and "body mind" (intention which desire of the body directs) toward yourself, and to be aware of existence affirmation and existence acceptance toward your "soul mind" and a higher direction.

Human eyes are seeing outward, human ears are hearing

Chapter 1 ☆ The Starting Point

outward, all five senses of the human body are pointing outward. According to those senses of the body, the brain evaluates the appearances, words, and eyes of others. Then the spirituality of the person analyzes them and directs the invocation of the consciousness and action based on motivation, thus determining the way we live.

So, human beings are in constant competition for other's evaluation, and strengthen the principles of competition according to evaluation and values as winners and losers, establishing a *negative spiral of social structure* such as academic supremacy, merit-based principles, and economic supremacy. It has been the social structure for a long time that winners were praised as the symbol of success and losers were despised like losers in life. However, no matter what your pursuit of status, honor, and wealth may be, seeking excessive physical world benefits will have adverse effects. For instance, if your brain becomes physically injured, everything you have worked for will eventually be gone, along with memories, and of course when you die, you will lose everything anyway.

Now, in the 21st century, more and more people are finally beginning to realize that we, as human beings, are paralyzed by this principle of competition which has been building through the 20th century, and that this principle of competition is an illusion and a big mistake.

We are also beginning to realize that we have created many negative legacies because of this principle of competition, and established wrong Self-satisfaction, and just ignored Self-improvement. As a result, we are now facing many crises such as environmental damages, family breakdown, chaos in the classroom, lack of social order, moral corruption, etc. The list is endless. Even religions, the spiritual world, and the philosophy of success, are busily engaged in the acquisition of excessive physical world benefits by *the selfish lack of virtue and by the hypocrisy of Self-satisfaction*. They consistently approach life by way of Self-realization and ignore Self-completion, which directs Self-enlightenment and spiritual evolution by virtue of unselfishness by Self-sacrifice.

We should not direct the arrows of our consciousness to the outside for acquisition competition, such as, superior or inferior, good or bad, rich or poor, higher or lower status, for other's evaluation. Instead, we should direct the arrows of our consciousness toward ourselves to evaluate our own Self-completion with gratitude and happiness based on Self-improvement for eternal purpose and values. It is very important to keep this theme in your soul memory and not lose your purpose and value for life.

In the 21st century, not *the Self-realization of excessive physical world benefits* (any conduct to seek those desires excessively), but the personal desire to make *Self-completion for spiritual world benefits* (any conduct for growth of spiritual consciousness entity), is the most important concept, and we can say that such a person is the real success.

The word PARAREVO is an abbreviation of Paradigm Revolution, and the ultimate paradox truth that makes this possible. It is a revolution of theoretical frameworks and values, which is the opposite paradoxical theory of the truth. Hereafter, according to the PARAREVO theory, all existing paradigms and dogmas which have been considered as good, such as theoretical framework and values of decency, religions, ideology, and economy will have been examined and weathered, and will disappear on a global scale.

1-2. The difference between remission and cure

The greatest threat of our lives, in history, is the microorganism. It is a pathogen called bacillus, i.e. bacteria and virus. Throughout the entire history of human beings, even in the religious cultures and science based civilizations, there has been an ongoing battle against the menace of this microorganism, which has terrified people because of life threatening epidemics such as typhoid, plague, cholera, poliomyelitis, dysentery, tuberculosis, and the challenging search for a cure has been relentless.

A bacteriologist, Louis Pasteur, discovered that all illnesses were caused by bacilli, which were external, so we understood that tuberculosis was caused by tuberculosis bacteria, typhoid was caused by typhoid bacteria, and so on.

These are called exogenous diseases, which are caused by bacteria and virus invading from outside the body. Medical science has nearly eliminated exogenous diseases, except for some endemic diseases such as AIDS and Ebola. Unfortunately, medical science has so far been unable to find cures for many internal diseases such as cancer, collagen disease, ALS, diabetes, angina, renal insufficiency, high blood pressure, etc., which are illnesses that seem to appear according to one's physical makeup.

But most human beings cannot distinguish internal diseases from exogenous diseases, and believe that modern medical science, which succeeded in finding cures for many exogenous diseases, will cure all illnesses, so they continue to visit hospitals to receive medicines. Why does this happen? I believe it is because of an inaccurate understanding about medicine. It is a big mistake to believe that medicine exterminates pathogens such as bacteria and viruses, against internal diseases.

For instance, anticancer drugs, frequently used in cancer treatment, are a good example. Even if a doctor says the cancer is in remission, because the symptoms have disappeared from CT and MRI images and blood tests, it will appear in a different location usually as metastasis. Remission is a condition that cannot be concluded as cured even though it is physically confirmed that the cancer is gone, because it does not remove the cause of the cancer itself.

There are 60 trillion cells and 110 trillion effectual microorganisms in the human body. So, it is not medicine that exterminates pathogens, it is enzymes, which the human body produces by itself, and effectual microorganisms along with a group of so called immunity cells, such as macrophages, natural killer cells, killer T cells, lymphocytes and white blood cells, used as a defense force.

When life on earth first began, the environment was very harsh. However, the cells and effectual microorganisms had the

Chapter 1 ☆ The Starting Point

intelligence to survive for the continuation of the species for 3.8 billion years, adapting with the changing of the environment. They have built wisdom to survive in the process of evolution, as "instinctive remaining consciousness," or "DNA consciousness." Therefore, human beings have survived by accomplishing evolution perfectly, constructing the collaboration system between cells and effectual microorganisms, and leading to coexistence, mutual prosperity, and symbiosis.

In the micro world of the body, we are directed to order and harmony in an attempt to complete the life activity with combined "DNA consciousness," the perfect wisdom survived in the 3.8 billion years, and the power of collaboration, the power to integrate. It will make a big difference in your life whether or not you believe the wisdom and the power of collaboration are involved in your own perfect body as potential ability.

1-3. Dimensional integration from individual purpose to entire purpose

Our life entity does not just live with the body, but is also composed of a complex integration of the soul, which is the spiritual consciousness entity.

Each cell has a unique consciousness and individual soul as it's character. For example, the soul of a cancer cell cannot be eradicated by physical management.

So, if you have cancer and have been treated by surgery or

chemotherapy, and the cancer is in remission, but the soul of the cancer cell still remains. Therefore, the cancer cell will reappear in another part of the body, spread by metastasis.

The soul assembles six trillion cells, each of which has the "personality consciousness entity," and creates one human body. For instance, the makeup of the liver allows it to only propagate liver cells, and only work as the liver. Liver cells do not change into stomach cells unexpectedly and do not work as the colon. If that were the case, it would be like a human being suddenly turning into a frog.

Regarding the structural arrangement of the gene DNA, the liver and the stomach are tremendously different from each other in information about the genetic code. Taking a daunting 3.8 billion years, the liver went through the process of evolution and became the liver in order to fulfill its roles and responsibilities according to the *law of the genetic chain*, and the stomach also had taken the same duration and accomplished evolution in order to fulfill its roles and responsibilities. In other words, the liver and the stomach are totally different in kind, regarding the genetic information.

The evolutionary process is directed to predominance for the purpose of the entire body, and the tissues and organs have evolved in order to fulfill their specific roles and responsibilities. That is, *the consciousness is the power, and the character points a direction, and always works as the vector to form harmony and order toward a higher level.* This power of consciousness and the direction of the character are always directed and ordered to a higher level and work to form the harmony of the entire purpose. So, in other words, the higher level things comprehend and restore the lower level things.

The cells are ordained to be tissues, and form a compound entity as tissues by co-existence and symbiosis, and the tissues are ordained to be organs and form a compound entity as organs. The consciousness of the organs is directed to the consciousness of the entire life entity and integrated into the entire purpose. So, the consciousness of each organ is unconditionally directed to the higher direction and works to form the harmony of the entire body.

With one human being forming the entire harmony of life, the life entity itself exists and is maintained. So, one cell in the foot and one cell in the brain complete their own individual purpose, role, and responsibility for the entire purpose of the human being. Therefore, the cell in the foot and the cell in the brain are given equal value for the entire purpose, without the distinction between superior and inferior, owning the equal existence purpose by completing the role and responsibility for the personal purpose.

Thus, ideally, the consciousness of each human being should be directed to the harmony and order for the family, consciousness of family should be directed to the harmony and order for the entire society, consciousness of the society should be directed to the harmony and order for the entire nation, and consciousness of the nation should be directed to the harmony and order for the entire world, so that global harmony and order is formed and peace and stability are established.

The roles and responsibilities of individual purposes can be directed rapidly to Self-completion for personality transformation and spiritual evolution by giving more priority to the entire purpose. It is collectively referred to as the *"principle of evolutional dimensional integration."*

1-4. The nature and individuality choose a path to health or disease

There is an activation of consciousness which is induced as totally opposite from the "principle of evolutional dimensional integration."

Cancer cells are representative of individual cells directed to the proliferation of disorder and formation of disharmony, enclosing a Self-centered and egotistic nature at the cellular level. A single cancer cell will eventually form an organization, propagate up to the organs, and destroy the harmony and order for the life balance. It will finally reach a destruction of life level and will cause the death of the individual life entity.

It is not DNA that determines the behavior of cells, rather it is the character of the cell that operates DNA, and the cause of health or disease is determined by the relativity of consciousness and individuality. So the information of DNA is just a direction for the result. In our life, consciousness is the cause and the subject, and behavior is the result and manifests as the object. The principle is based on consciousness followed by the corroboration of motive, words, and action. As a result of that trinity of consciousness,

Chapter 1 ☆ The Starting Point

motivation, and behavior, our life will manifest. This principle is called *the rule of "spirit is subjective and body is objective."*

Throughout history, there have been many times when one person has created horrific tragedies causing the destruction of order and harmony. Those incidents began with the breakdown of family, and spread to the society, the nation, the country, and ultimately, the entire world.

In recent years, typical examples are Hitler, who was a fanatical nationalist and ruled the country absolutely, and Stalin and Mao Zedong who ruled their countries as communist dictatorial nations. In addition, there are the religious dictatorial nations ruled by Islamic fundamentalists.

These are collectively called the *"principle of recessional dimensional domination"* or *"instinctive remaining consciousness."* It is an unexplained phenomenon that our combative instinctive consciousness, destructive instinctive consciousness, and dominant instinctive consciousness have been suddenly triggered. These consciousnesses are the unbroken chain in the evolutional process of surviving a poor and severe history. They have been built by "dietary desire consciousness" and "sexual desire consciousness," and are possessed equally as the "instinctive survival consciousnesses," by every living thing on earth.

Because the activation of consciousness toward evolution and the direction of the individuality are the central presence which has born the spiritual evolution and individuality evolution, consciousness and individuality form the collective entity as organization. The consciousness of organization and individuality then form the collective entity as the organs and society. The organs in turn, and each consciousness of the society, form the harmony and order of the entire life and entire nation under mutual interaction and mutual aid, and direct to the higher world system.

The consciousness of the entire life and integrity of individuality determines and directs vitality and life itself, as a single human being.

We can say then, that *consciousness and individuality are the vector to make order, and integrate and create respective peculiar energy according to the place principle that is derived by the vector and the related object, and transfer it to life energy.* In other words, the power and direction are constantly made order to the higher level and form harmony, by unseen influence.

1-5. "Surprising Phenomenon" and the effect of drugs

Our anxiety and fear about illness and death have been the driving force to produce various cultures and civilizations in a broad range of religions, sciences, and medicals. Especially in the field of medicine, the relentless search for longevity has led to the advancement of medical technology and, as a result, many new drugs have been developed and produced.

Health and money, which humans are trying so desperately to obtain, are actually opposite desires. This is another part of the health delusion which mistakes the means for the end. In Japanese,

Chapter 1 ☆ The Starting Point

the Kanji character for the word cancer is written as "the sickness with lots of articles". The health industry is in chaos, and the number of patients and medical expenses are steadily increasing in parallel. Despite reveling in the health industry, the number of sick people has never decreased, and the hospitals are flooded with patients. I believe it is because the true knowledge and understanding of one's own personal health care is very low and is the result of ignorance.

The purpose and role of medicine is the primer to activate immunity cells, effectual microorganisms, and the hormone system, which are innate in each person's body.

If the immune system and environmental adaptation ability function sufficiently, the mechanism and system provided in the collaboration of the human body immediately corresponds and combines in cases of bacillus invading from outside the body. However, if the immune system is destroyed and immunity power is decreased, it is not able to immediately take action against the invader. So, it is impossible to judge whether the bacillus invading from the outside is friend or enemy. As a result, the immune system ignores them and eventually illness appears.

There are autoimmune disorders, such as Atopic Dermatitis and sinus allergies, in which the immunity cells attack aggressively their own normal cells and tissues, due to rejection by internal discord. In these cases, they are not able to distinguish between enemy and friend.

When immunity power is decreased, it cannot protect itself against the outside enemy, and illness will appear. When our cellular immunity system is dysfunctional and sleeping, by giving medicine resembling bacillus as a false enemy, it makes a *"Surprise Phenomenon"* to the immune system and the immunity cells. For example, penicillin was produced from mycelium, which came from blue mold, because it is very similar to the toxin of tubercle bacillus. This Self-defense system attacks penicillin as a Self-immunity system and will exterminate the tubercle bacillus at the same time. Vaccine and vaccination were developed by utilizing this "Surprise Phenomenon," and by giving or inoculating bacillus (antigen, pathogenic bacteria) into the body within the maximum limitation volume of non-conducting disease, during the juvenile period in which no immunity antibody has yet been established, provides an immunity system in the body.

With the emergence of multidrug-resistant acinetobacter and pseudomonas aeruginosa, the antibiotics frequently used for inflammatory diseases in modern medicine, cannot give any effect or result. Recently, this is causing big problems, such as, hospital-acquired infections and the frequent occurrence of the phenomenon of people dying from infections after surgery. It is because during the juvenile period antibiotics are abused too easily for light inflammatory disease, so that tolerance against antibiotics is established and as a result, environmental adaptation ability is formed against the antibiotic in the body. In the end, the immunity function cannot establish "Surprise Phenomenon" and does not react anymore. In the near future, there will come a time when antibiotics will not achieve success as the main "Surprise Phenomenon." I understand, however, that it is an important role for life evolution in the process of accomplishing environmental adaptation.

In this sense, it is fundamentally wrong to think that drugs treat diseases. The purpose and role of drugs is to induce and prime, to bring out the "Surprise Phenomenon," which is the potential ability connoted in the body by the 3.8 billion years' wisdom and collaboration. There are many other remedies, such as acupuncture and moxibustion, massage, osteopathic massage, chiropractic, and osteopathy, which are using this "Surprise Phenomenon." By giving more stimuli from outside to symptoms and obstacles happening inside the body, the "Surprise Phenomenon" is led and extracts Self-remedy power and Self-cleansing action and reduces inflammation and nerve atrophy.

Health foods, and the toxicity in the substance propolis, are typical "Surprise Phenomenon." Propolis is a toxic substance which bees put on their hives to protect it from invaders. Taking this poison into the body causes the "Surprise Phenomenon" and activates the immunity system to protect the body from the poison. Because of incorrect information, some people take propolis every day believing it is just a health food, but it is gradually accumulating the poison in the body, and when it goes beyond the limits of the "Surprise Phenomenon," they contract cancer caused by the poison of propolis, and in the end, they will die.

Naturally, when the effect of the medicines and the health foods is greater, the poison they have is stronger, consequently, many people become unhealthy and get diseases such as cancer. These people, ironically, seem to be in a big rush to die. Health foods appearing in network businesses are especially bad, because they have the two-faced relationship of material greed and health greed. Like the word cancer in Japanese is written as "the sickness with lots of articles", networkers in higher ranks have a higher probability to die of cancer.

All medications, health foods, and alternative medicines are methods to bring out our potential power system, established by 3.8 billion years' wisdom and collaboration, by the "Surprise Phenomenon," and to restore natural harmony and order. It is not medicine or stimulus which cures illness, rather, it is the immunity power of Self-potential ability and environmental adaptation ability that cures illness.

Qigong, or chi Kung, is also one of the "Surprise Phenomenon." For example, when we send "chi" to plants, such as vegetables and flowers, they bloom out of season or become giant. Since we human beings are greedy creatures, we tend to think it is good for a plant to have many flowers and to grow larger vegetables, however that is not true.

The "Surprise Phenomenon" has been intensely incarnated in bad things, promoting confusion in hormonal and genetic information and causing panic in the ecosystem, so it manifests not normal conditions but abnormal conditions, remarkably. If a person has a big ego, doing chi-kung is selfish and is in the lower level in his/her spiritual dimension, so he/she can easily encounter the "Surprise Phenomenon." The abnormal phenomena, such as self-centered and disorderly cells, proliferate, causing mass outbreaks and huge anomalies to occur easily, because they do not care about other cells and simply increase as they please.

The "Surprise Phenomenon" also occurs in the natural environment. There was an era when the EM germ was used and prized, because it was a pioneer in natural, organic agriculture and was sold as "the way of the future" in farming. However, what is going to happen if we take a microorganism which has been raised in the soil and history in the southern environment and put it in the soil in the northern part of Japan, such as the Tohoku or Hokuriku region? Because of the process of evolution, when the unrelated microorganism is suddenly introduced into the soil, it is natural that panic takes place, accompanied with the "Surprise Phenomenon." The crops raised in this soil react to the environmental change so quickly that they bloom out of season, desperately fighting for the continuance of the species by bearing as much fruit as possible. However, the crops can bear fruits for only 2 to 3 years at best. After that, the soil becomes wasteland, barren and dead.

Because of ignorance about the evolutional process for the environmental adaptation, it was a stupid plan to throw extraneous cells artificially into the natural environment, driving it to a panic condition, exceeding the ability of environmental adaptation, and making the soil itself dead. It is exactly the same with the situation of over-vaccinating BCG and losing lives to tuberculosis. This is a bad example of using the "Surprise Phenomenon."

A good example of using the "Surprise Phenomenon" is slash-

and-burn farming. Burning grasses makes moderate "Surprise Phenomenon" inside the soil and it creates vital power there, which makes strong soil in a natural way. It is just like moderate moxibustion for the human body.

If 100 people eat a meal containing Vibrio cholera, all are infected with the virus, but only 2 or 3 people, which is less than 5 %, develop the disease. Most people have only light nausea and diarrhea but do not end up contracting the disease. Why is that? It is because the cause of illness is not outside but inside of one's own body. Since our eyes always see outside and our ears always hear outside, our consciousness is always stimulated by the outside phenomena. However, the true cause is not outside, but inside. Something outside can be a factor or motive but cannot be a cause.

We have seen made fools of by medicine myths and health foods. We should not so easily rely on medicine or health foods but instead, and most importantly, believe in ourselves, and always make our own effort to get the environmental adaptation ability and collaboration power for forming and maintaining the harmony and order to the surrounding environment.

Religion and the spiritual world are quite powerless but, of course, people in fanatical religious or spiritual groups would say that some people are cured. However, some people remained sick when I asked whether it was possible to heal 100 %. So, people who are cured do not have to be involved in any particular religious or spiritual group. Whether a sickness is cured or not depends on the person himself or herself. In other words, the fact that they happened to be in a particular group is purely coincidental, and has nothing to do with religious groups or anything else.

1-6. Boundaries between medicine and risk

Medicine and risk are like two sides of the same coin. When we deal with medicine, we have to be prepared to accept the risk as well. This is because medicine and risk are inseparably bound.

When we take medicine, we have to understand the boundary between medicine and risk, and take it within a safe range. We should not cross over that boundary carelessly and become dependent on the medicine. People with mental illness, such as depression, sometimes become dependent on medicine, such as anti-depressant drugs, and become Self-destructive and often take the most extreme path, suicide.

Since our own health is directed to Self-management by Self-determination, and Self-completion by Self-responsibility, based on the "rule of freedom," we should try hard to not so easily depend on medicine.

1-7. Common existing purpose and value of life

The common existing purpose and value of life for all human beings is to evolve ones spirituality, and to be released from the system of the earth, eternally.

When we human beings are born in this world, we know that

we will not live forever. So we should adopt a positive philosophy of death and straighten out our way of life.

In the 21st century, if we do not achieve the way of life which is rooted in the real philosophy of death, and do not find the existing purpose and value of life, the continuation of the earth life entity will be lost. The true definition of the philosophy of death is not to live with a paradigm based on the "earth logical evidence," but to live with a paradigm based on the "cosmological evidence."

People who live their lives based on the PARAREVO theory will never believe in one particular religion. They will have been freed from Self-righteous religious doctrines and framework of theory, earthly values, and momentary philosophy of death. Transcending race, environment, and the time axis, they will be living with the life in nature, and without any doubt or hesitation, feel joy and pleasure having accomplished coexistence, mutual prosperity, and symbiosis, with a sense of love.

The purpose of the 40 weeks of life in the womb is only the preparation period for a life on earth, and the purpose of approximately 80 years life on earth is only the preparation period for the spiritual life. The theories and values in this world will significantly differ if we leave the existing purpose of life and existing value in this world, and put it in the spiritual world after death.

It has already been proved in history that traditional religious paradigms, philosophy, ethics, morality, and psychology do not reach the truth.

Chapter 1 ☆ The Starting Point

Until the 20th century, mottos such as academic supremacy, economic supremacy and science almighty principle, were considered a symbol of a competitive society. We have been preoccupied with acquiring excessive physical world benefits and have left a legacy of misery to children of the future because of many negative spirals.

The mundane and ephemeral philosophy in our world regarding death, such as, everything is over when we die, or, everything will be gone, finished, has become common. As a result, unbelievable social phenomena, such as the increase in violent crimes by young people, family breakdown, domestic violence, sexual ethics, social dropouts, classroom disruption, refusal to go to school, and young people not being educated, trained, and employed has put us on an accelerated path of Self-destruction.

What is the purpose of this planet earth in the universe? What is the common purpose of life? And what are the roles and responsibilities of each individual? Those are not mentioned in schools, or social life, or even by parents. We should ask ourselves why we are the life entity on the planet earth, and what is our purpose in this life? How can we live our life without true purpose? It is like climbing Mt. Fuji without the purpose of reaching the top.

Even if there is a goal in an individual toward Self-fulfillment in this world, there is no common purpose for Self-completion beyond death. People who do not strive for Self-completion are not able to find the existence purpose and value. Words such as coexistence, mutual prosperity, symbiosis, and co-development, are only words, so the social structure without harmony and order continually repeats in a broken state. The most foolish thing we human beings are doing is living without finding any common existence purpose and value of life.

1-8. Cells complete the individual purpose for the entire purpose

Our five physical senses always point outside and use stimuli from outside as a guide, and decide the goal and purpose of life. Therefore, the consciousness continues to direct outside and pursue the physical world benefits.

According to Self-satisfaction, based on external evaluation, we are dominated by acquisition competition for the evaluation of others. This and the excessive desire for the physical world benefits will only serve to strengthen the *"bad competition principle."* I am not saying that all competition is bad. There is good competition as well as bad. Bad competition promotes selfishness and lack of virtue by the hypocrisy of Self-satisfaction, whereas good competition accomplishes selflessness and great virtue by Self-sacrifice.

In order to understand the universal system, we should direct the arrow to our inner-self and learn the truth of the universe from our own body's mechanism.

Our body is composed of 60 trillion cells and 110 trillion microorganisms (the cosmological number), and everything from a cell to the tissues and the organs exist to complete its individual purpose for the entire purpose of the body, according to the role and

Chapter 1 ☆ The Starting Point

responsibility of each. For example, each cell in the sole completes its role and responsibility of the sole as its individual purpose. By this, it holds and is given the value of the entire purpose, in common, by carrying out the entire existence purpose of one person's body. Each cell of the brain completes the role and responsibility of the brain as its individual purpose and holds and is given the value of the entire purpose, in common, by carrying out the entire existence purpose of one person's body. Thus, from the body's point of view, a cell of the sole and a cell of the brain hold and are given the same value, in common, for the entire existence purpose of the body.

Since an individual exists for the whole and the whole exists for the individual, and by perfectly coexisting with mutual prosperity and symbiosis, and being complete, they hold the integrated value to the higher direction in common as the entire purpose. The human body is the perfect collaboration. However, sometimes a selfish cancer cell appears and threatens to destroy precious and irreplaceable life.

The 20th century type society, with its huge class distinction between people, accompanied with the disappearance of "nucleus families," and destruction of the village society, the emotional system of community has been destroyed in companies, municipalities and nations and has undergone a transformation to mechanical organization. People become more lonely and obliged to be isolated from society, and young people with personality disorders are increasing in numbers like cancer cells, by their egocentricity and selfishness. On the global level, people feel that the entire society is being threatened and violated by fanatical terrorists and is being put in the crisis of possible extinction.

In the 21st century, we are consistently being encouraged to direct the arrows of life to our own self, learning from the body and making Self-affection, Self-affirmation, and Self-acceptance as a cornerstone, and accomplishing the role and responsibility of the individual purpose to family and the entire society.

1-9. Scientific reason and fluctuations of relativity

People who live the PARAREVO way unconsciously become not using the word *"why."*

In the world of science, generally speaking, reproduction and theory are emphasized, and it is important that scientists attempt to obtain proof by matching theoretical and empirical formula and draw conclusions after accumulating visible evidence. However, compared to the energy wave level that exists in the universe, the wave level of our physical senses is so small that it seems to almost not even exist.

The energy band wave level of radiant energy in our physical eyesight only has a range from 360nm to 830nm, which is like only one decibel (bandwidth) in a small energy wave, and infrared and ultraviolet cannot be seen with the naked eye. Seen relatively, from the energy wave level existing in the eternal universe, the energy wave level seen by the naked eye is such a small range that it is equal to almost nothing. So, from a cosmic point of view, I could

Chapter 1 ☆ The Starting Point

say that we human beings are like a visual impediment, so it is nonsense to discuss the existence of something by seeing it or not seeing it. Science still cannot even verify atoms and molecules, and continues its focus on the theory based on the theoretical method of the atomic model.

We should trust our own senses and emotions rather than scientific evidence. In the manufacturing world, there is an artisan's sensibility of craftsmanship, which transcends science. People who are at the forefront of science, such as doctors, physicists, etc., are faced with the limits of science itself and are coming to accept the need to transcend the framework of science very humbly and earnestly. There are many things and physical phenomena which cannot be explained by reason and the power of science only.

People living the PARAREVO way, first combine their experience and intuition, and feel the sensitivity and emotion subjectively, so that they become aware of the importance of receiving fact which is existence of phenomena based on matters and things, and building to the higher level of truth which is existence of consciousness based on SHINSEI. SHINSEI is *the existence that has the capacity to accept everything as it is, unconditionally and totally, based on free love. It is also the source of power that creates existence and directs every moment of now to a higher spiritual dimension.*

They also catch all things from all directions relatively, so that they never feel troubled regarding any one fact. For example, they know at the moment they affirm the good, the existence of bad is inevitably affirmed and manifested. Therefore, they can control their emotions subjectively without good or bad, without superiority or inferiority, without evaluation, and accept everything unconditionally, with happiness and gratitude, which is the basic concept of PARAREVO life.

All reasons and theories are not consistent, but relativized universally. All created things in the entire universe are forced to exist by the "rule of the relative original power." This is the rule of the causal power, inevitably and unconditionally derived from relativizing two or more things. This is caused by a slight fluctuation of imperfection.

There is no such rule of the absolute power. Contrary to this basic fact, the theoretical framework of science is considered as absolute, and attempts to reach one conclusion. So, it will cause a big fluctuation.

1-10. PARAREVO and the world of individuality wave

For people who live the PARAREVO way, the method to convey their thoughts to others is not based on scientific evidence. They don't need to convince themselves or others by explaining theoretically and religiously to obtain mind control. They trust and use their own nature and senses as the navigators of their own life, and judge their choices as good or bad, so that they bear Self-responsibility according to their own Self-determination. They never shift their responsibility or blame to anyone or anything, including their ancestors, previous life, or religion. They will never

Chapter 1 ☆ The Starting Point

believe in or depend on certain religious thought and values based on Self-righteous theoretical framework or physical world benefits. Everything regarding life is decided by Self-determination based on the "rule of freedom." To bear Self-responsibility to accept everything unconditionally based on the nature and sensitivity to feel the wave world, is the basic concept of the PARAREVO way to Self-completion.

The main concept for them is to feel it's energy wave rather than just believing it. Since they use their own nature and sensitivity to feel and catch the energy wave, and have established a firm Self-integrity for their way of life, they never believe religious doctrines, plausible theories of spiritual world, and success philosophy, or false and exaggerated advertisements such as organic product displays and the promise that supplements would bring miracles to your health.

No matter how well dressed, there can be falsehood, deceit, and fraud in words. However, there is no falsehood or deception in the energy wave radiating from the person himself or herself. Since they can feel the energy wave always there, the people who choose to live the PARAREVO way are able to live the individuality of their own lives without being fooled. They know that the existing purpose of life is to prepare for the life in the spiritual world after the physical death. They try to live to heal others by their own existence and provide them comfort and peace, feeling naturally the importance of the wave in sensitivity and emotion rather than in the importance of words. In the spiritual world, the moment they think, the wave of the thought is transmitted to others and there is no need for words.

1-11. PARAREVO makes bloom, endless creativity power

The fundamental attitude toward life, for the people who live the PARAREVO way, is to enjoy life with everybody together, more than anything.

Under the principle of competition, especially bad competition, such as that in the world of education, business, and sports, based on the earth logical evidence, we are used to competing against one another for everything, and only the winner can survive and be accepted by society. However, this kind of thought has limitations, and only produces unpleasant emotions. It is becoming increasingly clear that this way does not work well.

The 20th century type of philosophical theory, in which one who works as hard as one can is considered as good and right, will collapse and eventually fade away. The best results and achievements in living the PARAREVO way, are by creating a happy, fun, and active environment with joy and gratitude, based on love, and open each person's potential ability for achieving his/her goal, and to create the environment for each person to manifest as joyful, individual art. When such an environment is established, limitless creativity is born and synergistic resonance effect takes place, unbelievable epoch-making ideas and inventions, which transcend even the potential abilities, will be born in each person.

Chapter 1 ☆ The Starting Point

Since this produces tens of thousands of times larger output with small input, the PARAREVO way suggests that people do not have to try so hard but enjoying everybody's individuality can form the collaboration and open their own creativity. They are very active in the field of their specialty because they enjoy what they are doing, and therefore, increase their special knowledge, and will evolve being granted new values by building experience.

The relative fields of the way of life in PARAREVO are endless, and one never competes for the evaluation of others. It makes possible to manifest one's own desired art. In the way of life of PARAREVO, the individual art is not to criticize, evaluate, or compete with others. Since everybody's personality is different, the more important thing is that each person can feel always the best and the most wonderful. At the same time, in the way of life of PARAREVO, since the personality is multifarious, it is possible to create a huge synergistic resonance effect by exchanging information with each other, establishing a mutual support relationship between each other, talking about each other's art, and accepting the existence of each other based on love.

Therefore, people should not live with the hopeless theory of the principle of competition according to the profits in this world, ignoring the personality with theoretical framework and values of the 20th century type, but to live with the courage to decide their most favorite thing as their life work and live based on the belief with the individuality as the subject. That is the life of PARAREVO and it is the best way to manifest life as the individual art.

1-12. The way of life of PARAREVO establishes Self-evaluation

The reason people who live the life of PARAREVO never fall into situations which result in uncomfortable or unpleasant feelings is because they do not direct their consciousness to acquisition competition for the evaluation of others. The fundamental way of life for those who live the PARAREVO way, is to not allow the "bad competition principle" such as to fight or compete with others, into their life. On the other hand, people who live a way of life generally called "normal," unconsciously decide their way of life and behavior, such as manners and thoughts, by others judgments, because they are always worried about criticism and evaluation by others. So, they generally do not do things if they cannot receive evaluation from others, and only do things if they can obtain evaluation from others. They live their life for others and become secondary to their own evaluation of themselves and basically live the life of a lie, having fallen into the "good boy syndrome."

Since the way of life of PARAREVO clearly draws a boundary line separating oneself from others and establishes Self-integrity, they make Self-determination by their own free consciousness and establish a life style for Self-completion bearing Self-responsibility. At the core the way of PARAREVO life believes, that small power is not dominated by bigger power. It does not matter who is winner and who is loser, and no one ever measures people or is measured by people on merits of education, economic power, social status or wealth.

Chapter 1 ☆ The Starting Point

The paradigm of life based on the earth theoretical evidence of the 20th century, always directs the arrow of consciousness to the outside, so people fall into "victim consciousness" and shift the responsibility, blaming this person or that person, so that it only suggests a possibility of yielding to Self-hatred. And it leaves one vulnerable to intractable diseases such as cancer or mental illness, because of Self-injurious behavior caused by Self-denial, which leads to Self-destruction.

However, the lifestyle of PARAREVO, based on the "cosmological evidence," always directs the arrow of consciousness to oneself so that it suggests the possibility of Self-enlightenment and spiritual evolution by evaluating oneself humbly and modestly, based on Self-acceptance by Self-affirmation, and by Self-examination and Self-affection based on Self-verification.

1-13. Limitations of the paradigm of the theory of "right and wrong"

In the lifestyle of PARAREVO, the general evaluation of "right and wrong" and the borderline for the values are clearly respected in Self-evaluation and Self-responsibility. It is more important to make an evaluation toward one-self and value it subjectively rather than make an evaluation toward others and value it objectively. This way, the borderline separating one-self and others for `right or wrong` and the Self-integration, are clear.

Because of the values of "right and wrong" in the 20th century, we are judging of others through our justice system. If the justice system decides you win, then the system is saying you are right, and this is considered justice. People have lost the criteria to judge what to do and what not to do by their own decision with confidence. Trials used to be held behind closed doors by legal professionals, however, the jury system has changed to a citizen judging system and now people judge people to decide either "right or wrong." It reminds me of the old saying that *people who judge people on earth will be the ones to be judged in heaven,* and it seems that we are heading toward a very scary and sad situation.

The lifestyle of PARAREVO is to accept the existence of a person unconditionally, regarding their lifestyle and behavior, and never make criticism or evaluation. The basic stance of the lifestyle of PARAREVO, by drawing the borderline separating oneself and others and establishing Self-integrity, is to not make any emotional discharge or empathy for evaluation by others.

What if you are the only human being on the earth? Do you get uncomfortable feelings such as discontent and dissatisfaction toward the natural environment when it is hot or cold or raining? If there is nobody to reveal such discontent and dissatisfaction, you have to accept the total environment unconditionally. If you do get such feelings, it could mean that you are affected by mental disorder such as schizophrenia. If you are the only one existing in the world, it would be meaningless and purposeless to derive such feelings based on evaluation such as happiness or unhappiness, beautiful or ugly, and superior or inferior. Since people, in general, engage in

Chapter 1 ☆ The Starting Point

acquisition competition for evaluation by others, it could mean they have a schizophrenia type of mental disorder.

Establishing Self-integrity means to direct the arrow of consciousness to your own inner-self, drawing the borderline separating the "soul mind" and "body mind," making inner separation and directing toward "soul mind," and making the effort for Self-management by your own determination and Self-completion by your own responsibility.

Up through the 20th century, there was a history of schizophrenia-type mental structure, which has been dominated by the acquisition competition for others evaluation and the excessive physical world benefits. Repeating the struggles of "right and wrong," at the turning points in our history, has been the unfortunate history of this world. It seems that all struggles and wars have happened because of the conflicts between "right and wrong", and the differences of values. Still now, the fundamental causes of religious struggles and wars between Judaism and Islam, and between Catholic and Protestant, and ideology conflicts between capitalism and communism are the result of Self-righteous religious doctrines, theoretical framework of "right and wrong" by ideology and differences in values. Since all religions exist based on Self-righteous interpretation, they fight and blame each other, even in the same religious sects, develop theoretical struggles, and are preoccupied with exclusive speeches and behaviors.

In the lifestyle of PARAREVO, everything has to exist in each dimension, according to the "rule of the relative wave and relative original power" based on the spiritual dimension. Those who live the PARAREVO way understand, according to each spiritual dimension, that the existence affirmation of good is to affirm the existence of bad as the opposite extreme. Therefore, the concept of PARAREVO is, *accepting everything totally and unconditionally.* People who live the PARAREVO life draw the borderline separating "soul mind" and "body mind" by inner judgment and make Self-effort to establish Self-integration toward the "soul mind," so that basically they are not emotionally affected by the theory of "right and wrong." Because their consciousness is not dominated by this, they do not get those uncomfortable feelings. In the lifestyle of PARAREVO, the view and purpose of life in this world is clear. They have realized that this is a preparation period for moving to the intangible spiritual world. It is the basic concept and policy of the PARAREVO way to not create sorrow and ONSHU and not to leave them behind in this world, neither for oneself nor for others.

Our spirits descended to the earth, according to the "rule of reincarnation" by conception, based on the rule that "soul is subjective and body is objective." Every soul descending to the earth, the "prison star," is already a "spiritual sinner." We all have our own assignments and problems to solve, because of holding hatred inside. In order to solve and release them, we choose as our parents, those who have common problems and assignments in their soul.

As I mentioned earlier, ONSHU is the mental conflict between "soul mind" and "body mind." However, when "body mind" holds a dominant position, it becomes hatred. Since we already have hatred in our soul before we are born, it is very easy to create more hatred but it is very difficult to release it. However, we should work on releasing it during our life time in this world, because it is the preparation we need to be ready for the spiritual world. The relationship between perpetrator and victim is also clear to the people who live the PARAREVO way. They fundamentally understand, according to the rule of "spirit is subjective and body is objective," which one has more responsibilities for the assignments and burdens to shoulder in this world.

Our evaluation of "right and wrong," based on the "earth logical evidence," is interpreted only by the framework of general common sense, so it has a tendency to understand that the perpetrator is wrong and the victim is right. On the other hand, the "cosmological evidence" does not interpret based on the theory of "right and wrong," and understands that both perpetrator and victim equally share the Self-assignment and Self-responsibility to the circumstance, and the Self-effort to not create ONSHU toward each other by Self-determination, based on the "rule of freedom."

People who live the PARAREVO life understand cosmologically that forgiveness with love or punishment with grudge are left to one's own free will. They also understand that the important concept is to make Self-completion toward the higher spiritual dimension and to use one's own best effort to make Self-determination and bear Self-responsibility as the assignment for Self-enlightenment and spiritual evolution. Whether they take ONSHU as a fact and accept it with gratitude or not, depends on each person's spiritual dimension. The theory of PARAREVO is the method *to transcend ONSHU to the fact with love, to gain Self-determination and Self-responsibility to accept unconditionally and totally, with gratitude and happiness, and to make Self-completion with the truth of the higher spiritual dimension.* It is because emotion, either good or bad, can transcend theory and logic, according to the "rule of freedom," and so that love and ONSHU would transcend the theory of "right and wrong" and reach to creation or destruction.

It is very ironic and sad, that with the framework and values of the general common sense theory, the victim turns his/her consciousness into Ashura (demon) or Kichiku (barbaric) by ONSHU with strong hostility and hatred, creating and preparing the demon world by oneself in the spiritual consciousness entity, the soul, ends up going to the spiritual world where Ashura and Kichiku live. On the other hand, the perpetrator sometimes has deep remorse and repentance for his/her sin, and being penitent, dies as a virtuous person. Which is more appropriate as the Self-completion of the existing purpose and the existence value of life in this world?

People who live the PARAREVO life, fully realize that there are limitations to managing emotions by the theory of "right and wrong," and that the problems cannot be solved by that theory. Rather it has been repeating a negative spiral and chain of unhappiness.

In the 21st century, we have no choice but to go into the perfect collaboration period by the way of life of PARAREVO, integrating and not struggling with the theoretical framework and values of "right and wrong." In order to make this happen, we should practice the lifestyle of PARAREVO based on the "cosmological evidence," and integrate the entire world based on true love, transcending the theory of 'right and wrong' based on religions and philosophies.

1-14. Views of life and death by Self-determination based on the principle of freedom

The theory of PARAREVO is not saying that life-sustaining treatment is wrong, but suggests that every human being is given the freedom and the right to live, and at the same time, everybody has the freedom and right to die. I feel that one's view of life and death should be a personal choice, not a decision made by anyone else.

People who live the PARAREVO life consider the establishment of the view of life and death an important concept, and understand that the existing purpose in this world is only the preparation period for the spiritual world, and the position in the spiritual world will be determined in the final moment of death. They understand the meaning and significance to die more than to live, and have a great interest in how one's soul, the spiritual consciousness entity, makes Self-completion and disembodiment as the great finale in the final chapter of life. They understand that the position of the spiritual dimension, by which the soul is sublimated, can be very different depending on the timing and speed that the soul leaves the body and journeys to the spiritual world.

The requirement time for one's soul to complete disembodiment to the free spiritual world, releasing the persistence of the physical domination and ONSHU without attachment is very important, because it determines whether or not one can die with his/her mind at ease, allowing the soul to rest in peace.

The arguments for and against life-sustaining treatment and euthanasia without proper understanding and interpretation about the view of life and death would be different by establishing the true view of life and death. The theory of PARAREVO has raised an important issue regarding life ethics, i.e. whether it is right medical ethics to practice life-sustaining treatment and whether it is happiness or unhappiness for the patient, because the soul of the patient might hope to go to the spiritual world as soon as possible but cannot be released from the body.

It is time to discuss seriously whether it is right medical ethics or life ethics to be forced to endure anguish and suffering for many months and often years in this world, being a burden to many people, mounting up enormous medical costs, adding to the already high cost of health care, and in the end, leaving a negative legend until the moment of death. This problem even plagues the materialists, who generally say there is no spiritual world and souls do not exist and when we die, we all come to naught.

The lifestyle of PARAREVO suggests that we should direct ourselves toward Self-completion in preparation for going to the spiritual world. So, in case we are ever faced with a life threatening situation, we should make a will directing how we will be treated

Chapter 1 ☆ The Starting Point

when we face our last moments in this life.

If a person wishes to continue life in this world, to the end, receiving life-sustaining treatment even if it means nothing more than breathing, being bedridden, having no feelings, no joy, and having an intravenous drip injection, this person must plan to bear the burden of his/her medical expenses by himself/herself, according to the principle of Self-responsibility. If one decides on euthanasia, dying like the falling cherry blossoms, quickly, quietly, with beauty and dignity, without any pain in his/her last moments, and with gratitude for his/her entire life, then this is the motivation directing to Self-completion by the Self-management and Self-responsibility with Self-determination based on free intention, so that no one can intervene.

You might notice that I repeat Self-completion by the Self-management and Self-responsibility with Self-determination many times, and you might be tired of reading this. However, since human beings are very good at directing arrows to others, and not able to change the habit easily, I have to be persistent, by repeating these words in order to break this habit.

Many ignorant religions say that euthanasia is to be considered suicide. However, depending on the reason, whether it is an act of Self-harm based on Self-hatred and Self-denial, or whether it is Self-completion by Self-determination based on the motive of Self-affirmation and Self-compassion, by the virtue of unselfishness by Self-sacrifice, giving the entire purpose more priority, the level in the spiritual dimension, where the soul goes after death, will be greatly different.

In the lifestyle of PARAREVO, *it becomes an important concept to make Self-determination for Self-responsibility to accomplish Self-completion, and how and when to retire from life. This is the personal art, which is the final chapter and compilation of one's life in this world, by free consciousness.* The theory of PARAREVO clearly suggests that the 21st century type of medical ethics and bioethics is based on the true view of life and death.

1-15. Harsh environment shows the way of spiritual evolution

The ordeal of mental and physical pain gives the best opportunity to release the physical domination and direct you to Self-Enlightenment and spiritual evolution. Self-Enlightenment and spiritual evolution are to aim for Self-completion, bearing Self-responsibility for one's own determination, based on the "rule of freedom."

I understand that even Jesus was given the test for the final spiritual evolution, while on the verge of death, on the cross. Since the contents of the Bible have been interpreted and rewritten and adapted by human hands for hundreds of years, the facts may exist, however, in actuality, there is little to no truth anywhere in it. If the truth were to be known, it would be known only by the soul of Jesus, his own spiritual consciousness at the moment of his death on the cross, and by no one else. Salvation is not given by help from outside, such as believing in the Messiah, Buddha, or any religious

Chapter 1 ☆ The Starting Point

leader. The common theory with many Christians is that just believing in Jesus will give you salvation, but it will not.

The messiah of the spiritual evolution is the given environment and your own self, and depends on how you live the PARAREVO life based on the roles and responsibilities you imposed on yourself. Freedom is the fundamental attitude of the universe, so our consciousness is totally free whether we use our life for power, struggle, and destruction, or use it for love, harmony, and creation, based on the "rule of freedom" in the universe, however, we must bear all responsibilities by ourselves. *Freedom can be exercised when responsibility is secured, but freedom without responsibility is violence.* Whether Jesus bears the cross with emotions of anger, resentment and curse, or accepts it with full mercy, compassion, and unconditional love, it is the responsibility of Jesus himself to accomplish Self-completion by his own Self-determination.

The major point in releasing the physical domination and accomplishing spiritual evolution and transcending the harsh environment with love, is that *you must always try to create your individual happiness by your own personality, based on free love at this moment, facing directly toward yourself.* Based on the lifestyle of PARAREVO, this will determine the direction of Self-enlightenment and spiritual evolution.

1-16. Up through the 20th century, was the era of the "one-way method"

Now we are facing the time to revise our education systems for schools and families, even for society and nations, so we should drastically re-examine our theoretical framework and values as human beings.

Because of the competition principles such as academic supremacy, economic supremacy and the "science almighty principle," all theoretical frameworks and values have become complex and diversified and lost intrinsic quality for human beings. We are now reaching the peak of chaos and confusion in the mundane, material and momentary mental and social structure. Our good traditions and cultures have been destroyed and have disappeared without anyone noticing.

Because of the scientific civilization, television has become the center of life for many people. As a consequence, we have lost our communication with family members, children have lost their parents and family, and people have lost each other. This situation has taken us to an era of individualism without personal affection within families. This is especially true for children whose life style has become game-oriented. It is becoming harder for them to make conversation or have any communication with others.

We can take nutrition into our body by eating foods, however, the only way we can get nutrition for our soul, our spiritual consciousness entity, is by communication and conversation with family members and other human beings. When we devote too much time to TV

Chapter 1 ☆ The Starting Point

video games and computers, and are involved with machines all the time and lose conversation and communication with family and others, the soul will become malnourished and the spiritual mind will dry up. If we allow this to happen, we will become emotionally lost, mechanical, inorganic and maladaptive human beings with grave personality disorders.

Up through the 20th century, everything has been built by the one-way formula and the one-way dominant structural form in the family and society. For example, throughout the history of most of the world, inheritance bases have been constructed so that the oldest son will inherit the family business. This is based on the male's right of succession, and the family has been ruled by the vertical dominating structure under the authority of the father. In the social structure, based on authoritarianism, a high ranking man of power has legally organized the lower ranking weak by the pyramidal dominating structure, one-sidedly, and commanded societies and nations.

The central government ministries and agencies have been organizing the administrative systems by a bureaucratic dominating structure, and controlling everyone, from government officials to local officials, and commanding all administrative business. Even in the education system in Japan, it has been the norm that the Ministry of Education commanded the Board of Education, the Board of Education commanded each school, the principal of each school commanded teachers, and the teachers taught unilaterally to students. Thus, in Japan, each central government ministry and agency has reigned at the top of the vertical organization and used the rights to approval on their own terms by the "one-way method," and abused those rights by their own excessive desires. They have become slaves for benefits in this world such as income, wealth, and honor, and exploited public assets by privatization, legally making a revolving system for retired government officials to higher positions in private sectors. This is the male habit of the pyramidal dominating structure continuously passed down throughout the history of the "one-way method."

1-17. Mass media is the child of the "one-way method"

Television, as the largest media product of the 20th century, has gained the central role as the dominating structure, in the last century. Since most of the information received through the television is by the "one-way method," we as a nation, have been brainwashed to the unilateral theoretical framework and values, unconditionally, and have therefore had to accept them as though it was right. Thus, before we realized, TV reigned in the center of the family and has continued to reign as the center of society, pushing all power, and now virtually becoming the primary power.

Information broadcast over the TV, controlled by the "one-way method," has had a tremendous influence on society. For example, a domineering school student hit a more passive student. When the teacher told him to stop, he asked the teacher why and said he was just doing the same thing that he saw a famous comedian on TV

Chapter 1 ☆ The Starting Point

do, making fun of others and hitting them. Since parents who grew up with TV have raised their children by TV with no regulation, words like fool and idiot, and many worse words, have become commonplace, and children do not hesitate to use them. Why? Because they hear those words all the time on TV, those disturbing word ethics have spoiled the spirits of children and destroyed their personalities.

By this "one-way method" of TV broadcasting, lots of information has been given to us, unilaterally, and has flooded and expanded in disorder. People who have been brainwashed by TV insist on their freedom of speech and freedom of the press, however, this is freedom without responsibility, and freedom without responsibility is violence. Essentially, the press does not bear any responsibility to individuals, families, society or the nation. Mass media has fallen into economic supremacy, and is making irresponsible, chaotic, and false reports in order to gain audience ratings by the rating competition. Because those reports have been inducing undifferentiated sexual impulses and violent acts, it corrupts the sexual and social culture and spurs on distorted human formation.

This sexual disgrace and social ethics make sexual ethics and morals corrupt in the entire society, and spur on undifferentiated sexual impulse and violent crime among young people, and drive the society to various social problems and crimes. The true source of moral and social decay, such as drug-related corruption of youth and prostitution of young girls, pandemic explosion of AIDS, biker gangs, delinquency, social withdrawal, bullying and NEET (No

Education, Employment or Training), is mass media. In fact, the reason children do not listen to what their parents say to them, and the reason parents are not able to have an effect like the temptation and influence of TV, is because the words of parents are only the public nature of the family, but TV has the public nature of the society and the nation, so it has a stronger influence. As a result, children never listen to what the parents say but will listen to and accept what is said on TV, easily and unconditionally.

In order to protect children from the harm of TV, we have to be careful and not broadcast harmful programs irresponsibly, through TV. If people would like to watch silly comedy, they should go to a theater and pay their own money to watch it, according to the principle of Self-responsibility. Since education through the media has stronger influence than home schooling or school education, the nation and the people will significantly change if TV broadcasting will change. Freedom of the press and speech is fine, but freedom without responsibility is nothing but violence. The 21st century is the era in which unquestioned broadcasting ethics should be seriously challenged.

1-18. The 21st century is the interactive era

In the 21st century, because of the IT revolution, we will be shifting our direction to the interactive media era. With the growing popularity of the internet, we can exchange information with each other easily. I think the coming era will not be like the unilateral, "one-way method" like the 20th century was, and our society will become more mature and realize that the interactive information of the "two-way method" is the better way. With the advent of computers and mobile phones, it has now become possible to exchange information interactively, anywhere in the world, in real-time.

The TV era and the social structure of the "one-way method" of the 20th century is about to be changed drastically. However, if the information we are suppressing or exchanging with each other privately is not controlled correctly, it could lead to serious social crimes and juvenile delinquency. So, we should change our social structure from the "one-way method" to the "interactive method" as soon as possible.

For example, we should drastically reform the education system in our schools, and change the *"one-way method" of education* in which the teachers teach the students unilaterally, to the interactive cooperative growth system in which teachers not only teach, but learn together with and from the new generation students. We should also change the company systems. Traditionally, a superior pushes his subordinates to *work, unilaterally*. However, in the 21st century, we need to go a different way, a way in which the superior and his subordinates *work together, interactively and symbiotically*. Also, our society should not force the people, unilaterally, by the constitution and laws. Instead, we should change the social system so that the nation and the people co-exist interactively and harmoniously.

In the 21st century, we are unavoidably obliged to dismantle the right for approval type of system in which the central government reigns at the top of the pyramidal dominating structure, and has the power to make all decisions. So, we should now convert to a new system which will be a bilateral, globular type, integrating structure, the "interactive method" system. This change would be necessary not only in the central government but in various other fields including decentralization of local government. We have no choice but to build a society of co-existence, mutual prosperity and symbiosis.

According to the "rule of entropy relativity," interactive is also divided into two parts, one based on "soul mind" and the other based on "body mind." We must make structural reforms to the interactive social structure as soon as possible, but changes must be based on "soul mind". Because the "body mind" is ultimately connected to material desire and sexual desire, interactive exchange of information could create a dangerous society which would form a shadowy underground world.

Information should become more accessible to the right people who can use it with "soul mind." If it becomes more accessible to the wrong people who will use it for their selfish desires, because of the further IT Revolution, it will cause a serious and new national crisis and lead to the crisis of a new crime society.

Chapter 1 ☆ The Starting Point

1-19. Internal threats and the advent of crisis

We have so many problems in our society, such as increase in restructuring companies and people who are without jobs due to economic recession, increase in suicide and people who die from lack of care due to hardships of life and loneliness, increase in depression and panic syndrome due to future uncertainty. Also, violent crimes by younger people and family breakdown due to divorce are rapidly increasing. Those incidents have put a large shadow on society.

Economic problems regarding pensions, medical care, welfare and nursing are piling up, and still nothing has been resolved. The reality is that people are living their daily lives in the dark and just feeling their way along while holding on to anxiety and fear about the future. We are living with strange feelings of fear and anxiety which cannot be expressed in words. Now, we are facing an unprecedented critical point. Economic crisis, crisis in food, natural disasters such as earthquakes, extreme weather events, and global warming, man-made disasters such as nuclear war and terrorism, and the threat of a pandemic infection such as AIDS and new viruses, have gradually begun to appear as reality for each one of us. However, we need to realize that we are not only facing the *external crisis* resulting from outside influences, we must also face the *internal crisis*, which have resulted from inside our own selves and are increasing rapidly in the 21st century.

Also, the biggest threat and greatest danger for each of us is the incidence and mortality rate of malignancies such as breast cancer, uterine cancer and leukemia. Those are increasing among younger people, and regardless of age, the diagnosis of cancer is increasing rapidly. One half of the cause of death in the world now is cancer, and it is said in the medical world, that one out of every two people already have some type of cancer, and in the near future, that estimate may grow to as high as two-thirds. The biggest personal crisis we face now is contracting an incurable disease or an intractable disease. Regardless of the era, or the economic or environmental conditions, medical expenses and the incidence and mortality rate of cancer, intractable disease and foreign disease, are continually increasing.

Since the beginning of time, human beings have been obsessed with clinging to life in this world, and dreaming of immortality, while holding the anxiety and fear of sickness and death in their minds. Thus, we have been trying very hard to overcome those fears, and searching for immortality. As a result, science, medical science, and civilization have achieved remarkable growth. However, even with the advancement of medical science and the development of medicines, it has become clear that there are some diseases we can cure, but some we cannot. Since doctors understand better than anyone, that cancer, intractable disease, and some foreign disease cannot be cured by medicine, they have a stronger anxiety and fear of cancer than anybody else. In fact, when I asked them, if they were diagnosed with cancer, would they choose a treatment with pain and horrible side effects, such as surgery or chemotherapy, and would be very unlikely to cure their cancer. The honest doctors gave

Chapter 1 ☆ The Starting Point

me a definitive answer of no, they would not choose it. Sincere and honest doctors clearly state that whether cancer can be cured or not depends on the patient's *vital energy and fate*, and not because of the lack of the efforts of doctors, medical technology, or medicine.

Fate is determined by *what you meet, and vital energy is determined by belief and conviction toward the existence purpose and values in one`s life.*

When people who are diagnosed with cancer are told by a doctor that they only have a few months to live, the first thoughts they have, according to psychological statistics, are, *"Why me? What did I do wrong? Is this some sort of punishment?"* Then they go through a conscious repentance and Self-examination.

However, we are destined to not live forever and many people are realizing the vanity and emptiness of living in this world without purpose, meaning and significance. Since in actuality we are living to die, the fact is that more people are beginning to realize that the important issue is how we should live now to achieve Self-completion and to prepare for death rather than to just live life in the everyday manner we have been used to.

Nobody, including the government, doctors, and religions, know how to deal with increasing cancer, incurable disease, and foreign disease, or how to respond to medical and welfare expenses which have put enormous pressure on the national budget. We all wander about in the darkness without knowing our destination and without seeing anything, but just trying to feel our way along, holding onto fear and anxiety. The way to remove anxiety and fear of death and illness is to get *a true view of life and death and to understand illness and death correctly.* Understanding means to love, loving means to accept, and accepting means not to cause mental conflict and anguish. Not to cause mental conflict and anguish means to be released from Self-injurious behavior caused by Self-hatred.

In other words, *we should love even cancer, and then we can be released from the "body mind" which causes us to have uncomfortable feelings of hatred. Also, we can avoid Self-destruction.* To release your own hatred (malicious spirit, evil spirit and illness) by loving your own hatred (cancer), you must *grow out of ignorance and reach wisdom to find the cause of cancer.* Wisdom means finding the principals and understanding how *"the reason of the nature and the reason of the universe"* work. By acquiring wisdom, you can find the real purpose and value of existence, also you can clearly see the direction you should go, lighting the truth of the universe as a candle. When you walk in the light you can see everything without any fear and anxiety and you will find it possible to live in peace and happiness.

Since the Cosmic Bible is *the book of healing,* it will be the savior of the aphorism for those who are suffering from cancer, incurable disease and foreign disease, and those who have relatives and friends suffering from these illnesses. It will also help the people who have fear of cancer even though they are now in good health.

When you release the arrogant habits in the depths of your mind based on the spiritual dimension, facing the contents very seriously and understanding humbly, the cancer will be apoptosis (Self-destruct or regress).

Chapter 1 ☆ The Starting Point

1-20. Is cancer physical predisposition or mental disposition?

We often hear people say things like "cancer runs in my family" or "I know I'll get cancer because a close family member had it." The big question is this. Is cancer really a fatal genetic disease passed down from ancestors, or might the fundamental cause of cancer be something else? There are many families in which a parent has died from cancer, but the children have lived full lives and died of old age. On the other hand, there are many cases in which children have suffered cancer but their parents did not. In fact, it has been widely reported, in statistical surveys of people who had cancer that the cancer incidence and blood line do not match in the causal relationship.

The theory of PARAREVO suggests that the cause of cancer is not because of genetic DNA, but is caused by the individual's *mental disposition and/or personality.*

A major cause of cancer is the history of personality development, which is mind formation process, rather than the bloodline. The formation process for good habits or bad habits of mind is determined by the personality dimensions and values of people involved in the personality formation history, such as, what kind of parents, what kind of siblings, and what kind of family environment and friendships they grew up with.

People become extremely low ranking personality in the spiritual dimension if they are involved with people who have poor and ugly personalities, but naturally become higher ranking personality in the spiritual dimension when they are involved with honest virtuous people. This is called *the "rule of the relative wave in the spiritual dimension and the relative original power."* All power and energy in the universe is caused by or derived from this rule. Also, the motive of consciousness for mutation from normal cells to cancer cells and choice of motivation will become phenomenon and be manifested by this rule.

By the poor consciousness of those in the lower dimension with the egotism of Self-centered mind, cancer cells would be invoked by the relative wave with the consciousness of cells and the "rule of the relative original power." Then normal cells would transform into cancer cells, and the cancer would become phenomenon. Since the poor habit of mind is rooted in the history of the personality development, it would be impossible to find the cause and cure of cancer unless the formation process of your own "body mind" is analyzed and verified. The most effective ways and means are those which release ONSHU by *"regression into matrix."*

1-21. Threat of mental Self-poisoning

The fundamental concept of the PARAREVO theory is the principle of Self-responsibility. According to that principle, *illness is caused by yourself, so you are the one who should cure yourself.* Various data has recently pointed out that mental stress harms the health more than anything else. It has been found that internal toxins occur when we fall victim to uncomfortable feelings such as

Chapter 1 ☆ The Starting Point

discontent, dissatisfaction, deficiency, envy, jealousy, slander, abuse to people, impetuous behavior, anger, anxiety, and fear.

Here is an interesting case study. When we put the breath of an extremely angry person into a plastic bag, mix it with water, and pour it into a goldfish bowl, the goldfish float to the surface and die, immediately. This proves that when our consciousness falls to uncomfortable feelings we create strong and deadly poison by ourselves.

We can take care of exogenous disease, bacillus, with science and technology. However, there is no solution for Self-poisoning, which is the cause of endogenous disease, unless we bear the responsibility by ourselves.

Now we understand, by conclusive evidence, the difference between normal cells and cancer cells can be found in our own nature. However, we are unable to treat or cure the cancer unless we find the mechanisms which cause normal cells to mutate into cancer cells. In order to do so, we should examine thoroughly, the nature of normal cells and cancer cells, and clarify the fundamental mechanisms and laws.

By verifying the relationship between the micro world and macro world of the human body, and finding an interrelationship with both worlds relatively, we will be able to cure cancer.

1-22. Establishment of the true view of life and death

To overcome cancer, the most important thing is to *defeat your own fear and anxiety* of cancer. You might cry out in your mind and think that "It's easy for you to say, because you are not the one who has cancer." Yes, you are right. Nobody knows how you feel. When you are informed you have cancer, you might scream that "Why me? Did I do something wrong? Is this some kind of punishment?" And finally you turn your consciousness to the existence of yourself, unconditionally, for the first time. And yes, you are right. You are definitely being punished. The main reason you get cancer is because of your own mental disposition.

If a doctor is the cause of your cancer, you should depend on the doctor to remove the cause and cure your cancer, or if medicine is the cause, you should depend on medicine to be cured. However, the doctor does not have anything to do with you getting cancer. Therefore, the cancer is not the doctor's business, it is definitely your own business. Unless you become conscious of this and do not attempt to put the responsibility on others by falling into the trap of thinking that you are a victim and feeling sorry for yourself, and begin to take Self-responsibility, you will not reach any solution. Since nobody bears the responsibility for your fear and anxiety, because nobody has an obligation to do so, you may feel emptiness inside even though you ask for sympathy.

Even if you ask for help from religion or depend on health foods, you will not find a solution or treatment, because the cause of cancer is not in them. When people hear the false rumor that cancer is cured by religion, they easily become delusional and depend on religion. However, it is not the religion that will cure cancer, but it is the person himself/herself who will cure their own cancer by removing the cause. Your own cure can be triggered by anything. If one hundred cancer patients belong to a religious group, and all of them are cured of cancer by that religion, I would say it was the power of religion that did it, but I don't think that will happen. In fact, I think it is impossible, so you had better not rely on it.

Dependence means to yield to domination, and independence means to achieve freedom. There is only one way to be free from dependence. You have to find the real view of life and death to overcome fear and anxiety about illness and death.

1-23. Mechanism for mutation in cancer cells

The chakras have an important role and responsibility in connecting the consciousness and the body. Chakras link to the hormonal endocrine system and bring various changes in the internal environment by secreting the hormonal fluids. These are the triggers of the chemical changes of life such as motion, synthesis of body materials, maintenance of body temperature, bio-power generation, and bioluminescence. The hormonal systems are the triggers of the changes in the process of biological evolution, and it is DNA which has integrated the result as a chart (blueprint) of the life entity.

The mind, as consciousness, operates the hormonal systems and the hormonal systems operate DNA information. So, the real cause and subjectivity of the bio-changes is consciousness, and the hormonal systems are the information transmission glands, and it is DNA which manifests this information. Equal to only one drop from an eye dropper, this tiny bit of hormonal fluid has enough influence to change all information in an area as large as a 50-meter swimming pool, instantly.

The process in going from a larva to a chrysalis to becoming a pretty butterfly, and women's menstruation, menopausal disorders, aging, and illness, are all actions by working on DNA, in which the hormonal materials lead all effects accompanied with alteration and changes. The strongest impact to this hormonal system is the relationship between the chakras and consciousness.

When our consciousness fall victim to uncomfortable feelings such as complaints and dissatisfaction, Self-poison (the internal poison such as excessive hormones and active oxygen) grow, and "Surprising Phenomenon" occurs in the hormonal system, and causes panic and DNA damage, and this DNA's scar is the mechanism for change into a cancer cell.

The chakras are the *invisible spiritual organs*, which are in relative locations to the hormone systems and connect the hormone system with emotion and spirit, and have the responsibility to form harmony and order of spirit and body. So, when you balance your chakras, integrating your mental disposition and your body, your mind and your body will be cured.

Chapter 1 ☆ The Starting Point

1-24. Self-injurious behavior caused by Self-hatred is the root of all evil

If mental stress is the cause of disease, we should verify the fundamental cause of stress.

Our human eyes and ears are always directed outside, so that means our mind and consciousness are also directing toward the outside. We are always worrying about our appearance and behaviors, and evaluation of others. I could say that we are living a life like a weathercock. For example, you would decide your direction based on the other people's direction such as this person or that person goes or does not go. Your decision always depends on someone else's decision rather than on your own. Who are you, really? If you live your life without knowing the existence of yourself, you will end up living your life with no identity of your own. We measure things by the evaluation and values of others, and are always being controlled by other people's words and behavior. You always empathize to others and lose Self-integration, disguising your "soul mind" and playing like a pulp actor obeying "body mind", and you will live your life in the manner of a typical "good child syndrome." Being a "good child," if you want to do 10 good deeds, you would be carrying 10 burdens. By the same token, if you want to do 100 good deeds, you should carry 100 burdens. So when you disguise your "soul mind", the burdens will pile up more and more and eventually there will be an imbalance between the "soul mind" and the "body mind" causing Self-hatred and Self-denial, and finally end up with Self-destruction by Self-injurious behavior.

Everything you have done is for the benefits in this world such as status, honor, wealth, and for your own Self-protection. Even though you think you are trying to live your life for yourself, without noticing it becomes not the life you really want it to be. Why? Because you throw yourself into evaluation acquisition competition of others in order to get praise from others.

In Japanese Kanji, the word false is basically written as "person" and "for," so when you live your life for others, you are living a false life. Thus, by living a life without yourself as the subject, you would ruin your own precious and valuable life. By continuing a false life, lying to your "soul mind" and being daunted by your "body mind," you would be tormented by unpleasant emotions, and you would not be able to settle your "soul mind" and eventually fall victim to Self-hatred and Self-denial.

Since this feeling of Self-hatred is from your own negative heritage, you are not able to shift the responsibility to anyone, nor can you escape from it. Even though you want to, you will be unable to erase it. Since you are the one disguising your "soul-mind," you have to receive the unfortunate results such as illness or accidents, according to the principle of Self-responsibility.

The origin of unpleasant emotions is stress, and stress is Self-hatred, *which is the root of all evil.* This will cause all kinds of mental and physical diseases. Thus, *the typical illness resulting from physical Self-injurious behavior caused by Self-hatred is cancer, and the most common mental illness by Self-injurious behavior is depression, which could lead to suicide.* These are the typical illnesses of Self-destruction caused by Self-hatred.

Therefore, all causes are contained in your own mental disposition, and anything else can be a factor or a motive but cannot be a cause.

1-25. Crucial differences between cancer cells and normal cells

The smallest unit of life entity in our body is a cell. All others such as amino acids, proteins, and DNA are only material and hard to recognize as a life entity. The life entities in nature, such as animals, plants, insects, and even the single-celled organism, amoeba, have a very similar cell structure, and the energies from nutrients are stored inside molecules by synthesizing ATP (adenosine troposphere) from ADP (adenosine diphosphate) using energies obtained from a combination of light and oxygen. When energy is needed for motion, maintenance of body temperature, bio-power generation, and bioluminescence, they work as the life entities with the same chemical reactions of decomposing ATP to ADP and decomposing high-energy phosphate integration, and utilizing the generated energies.

We are the composition of 60 trillion cells. In order to overcome cancer, we must find the fundamental cause of cancer cells. If we do not find the cause, it will be impossible to cure or even effectively treat cancer. The main reason cancer treatment is the most difficult treatment in the history of modern medicine is because we have yet to find a clear physical difference between cancer cells and normal cells. If there is an obvious physical difference, a remedy for cancer would have already been developed, as we have done to defeat exogenous bacillus (viruses and bacteria) by vaccines and antibiotics.

It is difficult to identify cancer genes at the DNA level because a slightly changed cell proliferation gene is not necessarily a cancer gene. In fact, since similar genes exist in normal cells, immune cells have trouble distinguishing between normal cells and cancer cells, and overlook them without recognizing them as an enemy.

Unless we understand how and by what causes, the normal cell proliferation gene achieves mutation to the abnormal cancer gene, cancer treatment will be very difficult because modern medicine is not able to find the essential underlying cause of cancer, and only treats the symptoms not the cause.

Now I would like to clarify the fundamental cause and essential mechanism for the real cause of cancer by comparing cancer cells and normal cells. We should distinguish clearly the subjective cause and the objective result to cure cancer from its origin by verifying the crucial difference between normal cells and cancer cells.

We cry because our heart is sad, but we are not sad because we cry. We laugh because our heart is happy, but we are not happy because we laugh. When we examine cause and effect in this way, the cause is a state of invisible consciousness and the result is visible phenomenon on the body, so we can understand now that the invisible world can make phenomenon and manifest it to the visible world. External facts are not the cause of cancer. It is the

Chapter 1 ☆ The Starting Point

internal facts, such as mental stress, which result in the physical manifestation of cancer.

The crucial difference in normal cells and cancer cells is *the mental disposition* consciousness, which every cell holds. The consciousness of normal cells holds the mental disposition and will to try to form harmony and order directed to co-existence, co-prosperity, and symbiosis. On the other hand, the consciousness of cancer cells holds *the mental disposition of Self-centered type of greedy egotism* which multiplies and expands disharmony and disorder endlessly, stretching the blood vessels around in all directions, and taking nourishment from the blood, as if they do not care about other cells at all and just proliferate by themselves. As a result, the cancer cells destroy the harmony and order for the entire life, taking away and destroying the life entity itself, eventually leading the entire life to death, and at the same time, destructing themselves together with the life entity. Cancer cells hold *the mental disposition of the Self-destructive type of Self-injurious behavior.* This is *the real toxicity of cancer cells.* They never hold the toxicity physically but hold the toxicity in the mental disposition of the cells themselves, and this is the definitive difference between cancer cells and normal cells.

The Kanji characters for *illness* in Japanese *are written as sickness and mind, therefore illness comes from the mind.*

When our "soul mind" is no longer able to control our "body mind," the result is that a criminal act would be manifest in reality. The same thing will happen to our cells. The main thing that causes normal cells to mutate into cancer cells is when our "soul mind" is no longer able to control our "body mind" in the spiritual consciousness entity of the cell. As a result, physically, the tumor suppressor gene is no longer able to control the cancer gene, and the cell becomes cancer.

The same things happen in our consciousness. We have our mind world in our consciousness, and there are two conflicting minds, which are the "soul mind" and "body mind." When our "soul mind" is superior, we can spend the day calm and in peace, forming harmony and order. On the other hand, when our "body mind" is superior, we become restless and tormented by negative feelings such as dissatisfaction, envy, jealousy, and anger.

As you can see, all functions are in this mechanism. No matter whether it is good or bad, all are based on the rule of "spirit is subjective and body is objective," and directed to the entire purpose from genes to cells, tissues, and organs.

We human beings have similar appearances, facial structures, and bodies, but each person's mental disposition is entirely different. So, even if a person is greedy, he/she does not have 10 hands, and even if a person arrogantly thinks he/she is smarter and has a higher education than others, he/she does not have 10 heads. If such a world of the inner consciousness is clearly manifested in the external appearances, it would be very easy to understand and no one would like to be involved with or even approach a person who looks like the devil. There are some people who have the devil's face but an angel's mind, and there are some people who have an angel's face but the devil's mind. So, we can never judge another person by the face, appearance, status, or wealth whether he/she is good person or not.

Eradicating crime and incidents from society is just about as difficult as treating cancer. As the PARAREVO theory pointed out, *invisible mental disposition is the real toxicity*, so that makes cancer treatment difficult.

The cause of cancer is mental rather than physical, although there could be various factors including those from inside and outside. If a person has cancer and truly wants to cure it, that person has to cure the negative mental disposition of his/her propensity of mind, such as envy, jealousy, anger, anxiety, and fear. Those negative feelings are caused by shifting responsibility by the victim consciousness, based on the physical world benefit such as the desire for possessions and domination. If a person just keeps saying, with a high and mighty attitude, that he/she does not have an arrogant mental disposition, that person would just be giving up his/her life to cancer. The mental disposition is the sub-consciousness from a past life, and personality is the apparent consciousness after birth in this world. I will explain in more detail in the second chapter.

It is important to change the personality by changing the mental disposition, according to the "rule of preservation by inscription." However, the mental disposition from past life has a bigger effect on a person's consciousness than the personality.

You might wonder why such a nice person got cancer. It is because even though the person has a nice personality, his/her *mental disposition*, which is the person's problems and assignments, carries forward from past life. So, although one has a nice personality and has been working to change his/her mental disposition from past life, if the change is not complete, the unchanged part will manifest unless the person offset the negative mental disposition. To accomplish this, we should approach our own problems and assignments, including those from past life, and make the effort to change the mental disposition of our soul's propensity toward negativity.

Everything happens according to the principle of Self-responsibility based on Self-determination. Even though you may be a totally innocent victim or something unexpected and unfortunate happens, the cause is inside yourself, so if you do not have any direct cause for cancer in this current life, but it exists in you from a past life, it is the result of the consciousness directed to the "body mind."

You might be very shocked to find that such a negative thing exits in yourself. However, you should not turn your eyes away from the fact and should clean up the mental habit from past life by the virtue of unselfishness with Self-sacrifice, and accept the fact as it is with gratitude and happiness. Since each person's assignment is how to accept the phenomenon of cancer, if he/she can direct his/her cancer to creation and development rather than illness and death, cancer itself will become a very meaningful phenomenon to that person.

In the universe, everything is based on love. Becoming ill is the awareness of one's sinfulness and foolishness. We do not become ill to die, but through illness we can approach the spiritual revolution

Chapter 1 ☆ The Starting Point

to a higher spiritual dimension. Death is our ultimate destiny, so the important thing for us is to accept our own sin from past lives with gratitude and happiness.

Cancer can't be treated using the physical treatment, which approaches cancer from the body. To cure cancer, we should use the mental treatment which approaches cancer from the spiritual consciousness entity, the soul.

When people die, we can cremate the body, but it is not possible to burn the spiritual consciousness entity with fire in this world. It is possible to remove the cancer cells, but it is impossible to cut the spiritual consciousness entity of the cancer cells, just as it would be impossible to cut out the mental disposition of the person in which the cause of cancer exists, by physical surgery. Even though we remove the cancer by surgery, or use radiation therapy or chemotherapy to attack the cancer cells, it just offends the cancer. Although it may seem the cancer is in remission, with a physical examination such as CT or MRI and blood tests, it will appear in new and different locations with increased numbers, since the spiritual consciousness entity of the cancer remains as it is.

In medical terms we say that the cancer is metastasis, which is based on the rule of "body is subjective and spirit is objective." However, the PARAREVO theory recognizes it as a new appearance based on the rule of "spirit is subjective and body is objective."

Our life entity is not only composed by the physical body, but composed with comprehensive integration entity with the soul, the mental and spiritual consciousness entity. It is the same with our cells. Each cell has a consciousness which is its own unique character, and the will to complete its existence purpose and existence values. In fact, the liver only proliferate liver cells and only performs the role and responsibility of the liver, so it never suddenly metamorphoses into stomach cells, and never works as the lungs.

Regarding the structural arrangement of the gene DNA, the information of genetic code of the liver and the stomach are tremendously different. Through 3.8 billion years, an astoundingly long time, the liver has become the liver through the process of evolution in order to fulfill the roles and responsibilities as the liver, and so has the stomach. The process of evolution is oriented to complete the existence purpose for the entire body from each organ, to tissues and cells, and all life entities ranging from the original life entity, bacteria, to humans, had accomplished the life evolution through 3.8 billion years in order to fulfill the roles and responsibilities of each.

Thus, *the consciousness is individuality, and the will directs the existence purpose and values to complete, and always evolves to form the harmony and order toward the higher level.* This individuality and will are directed to the higher level based on the "principle of dimensional integration."

1-26. The "principle of dimensional domination" based on the rule of "body is subjective and spirit is objective"

According to the "principle of dimensional domination" in the earth star, *lower-dimensional things always dominate higher-dimensional things, so that higher-dimensional things are constrained by lower dimensional things. And lower-dimensional things are always attempting to increase discord and chaos, which leads to inconvenience and destruction.*

Therefore, as the life entity of the earth, *the lower-dimensional bodies always dominate the higher-dimensional spiritual consciousness entities, the souls, and the higher-dimensional spiritual consciousness entities are always constrained by lower-dimensional bodies and lead to inconvenience and discomfort,* according to *the "principle of dimensional domination" based on the rule of "body is subjective and soul is objective."*

As the "principle of dimensional domination" of cancers, *Self-centered and greedy cancer cells dominate normal cells and by stretching blood vessels in all directions, taking nutrients from the blood, and propagating randomly, they continue to form discord and repeat disordered cell divisions, and destroy the harmony and order for the entire life and bring the life itself to destruction.* This mental disposition is the true toxicity of cancer cells.

The economy is the blood of the world, and capitalism is the ideology theorized, based on greedy nature. Cancer-like companies and organizations that have been produced by this ideology stretch the blood vessels of the financial network all over the world and take the economy as the blood and exploit them greedily. It is reality that a small number of greedy people own most of the world economy, and most of the people in the world are suffering from poverty. Those greedy nations, ironically, have an extremely high rate of cancer incidence and mortality by cancer compared to the proportion of the population.

In the Japanese economy, the financial resources like taxes paid by the sweat of taxpayers are mostly taken by the cancer cell-like organizations such as the National Medical Association and the Ministry of Health, Labor and Welfare, and a huge tax is consumed as medical expenses. They have taken the nation as hostage, and are forcing people to depend on the public health insurance system, and are making laws and legalizing systems in order to protect vested interests of doctors. In other words, they have put a dominating rope called medical curse around the people.

Since medicine is related to life, the nation and government do as the National Medical Association says. It abuses the preferential tax system in the medical jurisprudence, unlimitedly deriving the tax as the nation's blood, openly constructing the mechanism that the blood tax will never be returned to the nation and systematized it in the medical site and the society.

Greedy doctors who preserve vested interests, own a luxury homes and luxury cars, and enjoy a life of gaudiness and gluttony including sending their children to expensive private schools. Since such greedy doctors treat greedy cancer cells, the mechanism and system they were supposed to restrain have continued unbrokenly,

Chapter 1 ☆ The Starting Point

so that the national financial source is facing an unprecedented crisis and falls into serious injury, like dying cancer patients.

The same thing that cancer cells are doing in the micro world of the human body is happening in the macro world of human being.

As the "principle of dimensional domination" in dictatorship countries, *a lower-dimensional greedy dictator always dominates the nation, and the people are deprived of the life and property by the dictator and a small group of the privileged, and they even restrict their rights and the freedom to live.*

The world had an unfortunate history when a coward who inherited the lineage of the Jewish millionaire, Rothschild, suddenly mutated, like cancer cells, as Hitler, and organized a cancer tissue, the Nazi party. Then he attempted to annihilate his own blood line, the Jewish people. The Nazi party eventually expanded its cancer tissue to the nation and kept expanding its cancer tissue, invading all of Europe. We have many unfortunate and sad histories which were brought about by one single dictator who destroyed the order and caused a breakdown of the harmony from families to societies, to ethnic groups, to nations and the entire world. In recent years, representative examples are North Korea's fanatical communist dictator, and indiscriminate acts of terrorism by Islamic fundamentalists.

In the structural power of the Japanese bureaucracy, the national administration and local governments are always dominated by regulatory control because of the greedy lust for status, material, and reputation by a small group of avarice bureaucrats with vested interests, and with their cunning interests and desires, exploit the rights of the people and bleed tax unconditionally. Since this Japanese bureaucracy is the most toxic and formidable cancer-like organ to treat, the reforms for administration and public finance and civil service are proceeding so slowly that there seems to be no progress.

1-27. The "principle of dimensional integration" based on the rule of "spirit is subjective and body is objective"

It is hard to cure cancer unless the treatment is in accordance with *the "principle of dimensional integration" based on the rule of "spirit is subjective and body is objective."* As the "principle of dimensional integration" in the universe, *the lower-dimensional things are always embraced to the higher-dimensional things, and the higher-dimensional things integrate the lower-dimensional things to a higher level, constantly striving to form the harmony and order, and directing to freedom and creativity.* For the life evolution, according to *the "principle of dimensional integration" based on the rule of "spirit is subjective and body is objective," the lower-dimensional body is embraced into the soul, the higher-dimensional spiritual consciousness entity, and the soul integrates the body to the higher level and directs it to the real freedom and spiritual evolution continually attempting to form the harmony and order.* The rule of "spirit is subjective and body is objective," the fundamental principle of the universe is that *personality of mind and spirit of soul are the*

Chapter 1 ☆ The Starting Point

subject and the cause, and the body and materials are the object and the result.

In the human body, according to the "principle of dimensional integration", *all cells, tissues, and organs are always directed to the higher entire purpose and try to form the harmony for the entire body.*

The consciousness of cell is directed for the tissue and form the compound entity called the tissues, with co-existence, co-prosperity and symbiosis, the consciousness of the tissue is directed to, and form the compound entity called the organs. The consciousness of the organs is directed to the entire body, and by being integrated to the existence purpose and values of the entire body, the entire life's activities should be completed.

One cell of the sole and one cell of the brain complete each role and responsibility of the individual purpose in order to complete the entire purpose of each human being. Therefore, the cell of the sole and the cell of the brain equally hold and are given the existence values in common by completing the role and responsibility of the individual purpose for the entire purpose. When you see from the entire purpose, it doesn't matter whether it is a cell of the sole or a cell of the brain, everything is equal and there is no difference in the merit or evaluation of values.

Thus, essentially, the consciousness of each human being should be directed to the harmony and order for the family, and the consciousness of each family should be directed to the harmony and order for the entire society. Then the consciousness of the society should be directed to the harmony and order for the nation, the consciousness of the nation should be directed to the harmony and order for the world, and will then be able to sustain the harmony, order, and stability of the world.

Therefore, by each consciousness and will, accomplishing the role and responsibility of the individual purpose and giving the entire purpose more priority over the individual purpose, it is possible to recover or form the harmony and order. By completing the role and responsibility of the individual purpose, it will be possible to hold equally the existence values of the entire purpose in common and form the perfect collaboration globally. Based on this rule, it becomes possible to convert the consciousness and will of the cancer cells, rapidly, causing them to apoptosis (suicide).

1-28. Individual and whole are based on the "chain of responsibility system"

One cancer cell will form a tissue which will eventually extend to the organ. When the order and harmony for the organ is broken, it will affect the entire life and finally will reach total life destruction, the death of the individual life. This is based on the "chain of responsibility system" of life, which is, *an individual is the whole and the whole is an individual.* An individual carries the responsibility for the whole by accomplishing the principle of free responsibility, and the whole shoulders the responsibility to the individual by bearing the entire responsibility.

Chapter 1 ☆ The Starting Point

As I mentioned earlier, the smallest unit of a life entity is a cell, and DNA is only a material. It is not DNA which determines the behavior of cells. According to the "principle of dimensional domination," it is the acquisitive consciousness of the individual person, the consciousness of the whole, makes the change of the consciousness of the cell, the individual consciousness, to the acquisitive consciousness and changes DNA, which results in mutation of the normal cell to cancer cell. The problem is not with the cancer cell itself, but with the person, according to "the chain of responsibility." The consciousness and intention are the cause and the subject, and the mutation of DNA is only the result and the object.

By our actions, consciousness and intention are the cause and the subject and the words and deeds become phenomenon as the result and the object. So, we could say that all our actions are based on our consciousness supported by our intention (motivation). Thus, consciousness, intention and action, are the trinity of result to manifest all things. Consciousness is the source of the relative original power which puts the "soul mind" and the "body mind" in motion, and intention directs motivation. Consciousness is power and intention is direction. We call this vector. By this vector our actions are manifest.

We must distinguish clearly between "soul mind" and "body mind" which are connoted in each person's consciousness, according to the "principle of dimensional integration" by internal separation, based on the rule of "spirit is subjective and body is objective," and convert the quality of the consciousness to the higher dimension by directing to one's "soul mind." The "soul mind" and the "body mind" exist simultaneously, but we should try to direct our consciousness to our "soul mind" not to our "body mind."

This makes the qualitative conversion of the spiritual consciousness entity of the cancer cell by directing it to the higher direction, the entire purpose of the body, not to the individual purpose of the cell, and transforms the nature to normal cell. Otherwise the cancer cells will seem to appear freely anytime and in any organ, as if they are spreading. Because of the structural arrangement of the gene, stomach cancer spreading to the liver or lungs is impossible. This is because the genetic information of stomach, liver, and lungs are different in the process of evolution in 3.8 billion years, so it would be like a caterpillar changing into an elephant instead of a butterfly.

The cause of cancer is not visible cells but in the invisible mental disposition itself. So, there is no logic in the theory that cancer cells metastasize to different organs or viscera based on the rule of "body is subjective and spirit is objective." Conversely, if that logic were justifiable, when cancer cells are removed, cancer should be cured and completely disappear at that point rather than going into remission.

What causes normal cells to become cancerous is not metastasis of cells, but is the mental disposition of the person himself/herself. So curing cancer with treatments such as surgery, anticancer drugs or radiation therapy is impossible. Unless the mental disposition of the person is changed, normal cells will change to various cancer cells freely and appear as cancer in every sort of organ and viscera based on the "chain of responsibility system" of life.

When we can understand this fully, cancer treatment will not be so difficult. We are able to approach cancer cells by spiritual consciousness revolution and can also solve the cause rather than approaching them by physical treatments.

We should try to change our consciousness by ourselves based on the "chain of responsibility system" of life. This will change the character and mental disposition of the cancer cells. As a result, cancer will be directed to existence denial and reach to apoptosis and will finally disappear.

With the PARAREVO theory, we are putting the value beyond a life-or-death crisis, and this same concept can challenge cancer cells. So we understand that it will entice cancer cells to pass away at ease and will allow the spirits of the cancer cells to go to the world of light. When we perform the treatment based on love, cancers will decide their own fate by themselves, whether by apoptosis or qualitative transformation to normal cells.

1-29. Sickness is the "phenomenon of love confirmation"

By verifying the mechanism that transforms normal cells into cancer cells, it will be possible to transform cancer cells to normal cells.

Cancer or any other kind of illness is the "phenomenon of love confirmation."

For example, how would you feel if you are working very hard in your job but your superior ignores your existence and forces you to do various things unilaterally, or gives you unfair tasks and treats you poorly? Do you want to contribute to that person and work with him? You might think you would like to revolt. What if you ignore your lungs and stomach and force them to bear burden unilaterally, by smoking, gluttony, and/or excessive drinking. Don't you think your organs and viscera would complain to you?

Often, children intentionally do some bad thing that makes their parents angry. This is a way to draw the parent's attention when they want to ensure the love of the parents. By the same token, the motivation of illness starts from an impulsive verification act for love and it will manifest as illness if you are not aware of it. Illness sends signs to you before its onset, however, if these signs are ignored, there will be no choice for it but to appear as illness. In other words, it manifests as illness, directing to Self-injurious behavior, as a last resort.

We should understand the psychology of this illness with Self-repentance, and accept the existence of the illness, unconditionally and entirely, with gratitude and consciousness of repentance, based on love, and direct ourselves to Self-enlightenment and spiritual evolution with the real view of life and death.

Chapter 1 ☆ The Starting Point

1-30. Sickness is Self-injurious behavior caused by Self-hatred

Based on the PARAREVO theory, the concept of physical and mental illness is defined as; *it is caused by the mental disposition of Self-hatred and manifested as a result of Self-injurious behavior.* It will be impossible to solve this problem unless we verify why human beings fall victim to Self-hatred and Self-denial. The personality formation history, which is the mental formation process of each person, is the origin of the fundamental cause of Self-hatred and Self-denial.

The personality formation history is *the shape of mind*, and the shape of mind is derived from the *mental history* of each person, which is formed by the consciousness formation based on experiences such as family environment, school environment and social environment.

There are many different family environments, and various family environments form the shape of each person's mind based on the personality formation history. A person who is born to poor parents and raised in an inferior family environment, and a person who is born to loving parents and raised in a family environment filled with love and freedom, would be totally different regarding the personality formation history, and their personality spiritual dimension and mental disposition will be different...exactly opposite.

The fundamental *nature of the cause* of Self-hatred and Self-denial is connoted with the consciousness as latent ONSHU of *parental-hatred and parental-denial*, because they could not receive *the ideal love* from their parents. For example, family environment with physical abuse like domestic violence and sexual abuse, adopted or illegitimate children who are not able to receive love from their birth parents, single-mother, single-father or orphans because of divorce or family breakdown, greedy family with blind love such as education supremacy principle, or etc. The vertical relationship of the birth parent and child is one of the important factors of the PARAREVO theory which releases ONSHU. This PARAREVO theory needs more understanding, so I will explain later in the next book why this vertical relationship is so important.

The personality formation history begins at the moment an ovum accepts a sperm. At that moment a soul inhabits the ovum and emits a light of the life energy wave. Children who are born as twins, triplets, etc. come from one ovum, and each child has a separate and different soul consciousness. The reason is because that specific ovum is inhabited by more than one spirit. This proves that the physical fertilized egg is not the cause, but the numbers of spirits inhabiting the egg is the cause, based on the rule of "spirit is subjective and body is objective."

If the cause is in the fertilized egg, then in the case of sextuplets, six fertilized eggs and six placentas (one for each child) would be needed. Even in the case of identical twins, or non-identical twins, there is only one fertilized egg and one placenta.

Nothing is different for identical or non-identical in the mechanism or the system that a woman becomes pregnant according to the rule of "spirit is subjective and body is objective." Spirit, the soul of the unborn child, comes first and because of the soul, the body will be formed. Unborn children prepare for life on the earth, forming mind and body, together with the mother's spirit. The existence purpose and existence value of prenatal life in the 40 weeks is only a preparation period for a healthy and meaningful earth life, forming a healthy mind and body in the womb.

According to the rule of "spirit is subjective and body is objective," the spiritual consciousness entity of an unborn child has inborn nature (the habit of the consciousness based on the spiritual dimension of the soul, which has been built in former past lives). The experience in the 40 weeks of prenatal life, whether it is a poor environment or a good, love filled environment, will determine whether the child will have a fortunate or unfortunate, healthy or unhealthy, life on this earth. This is a very important period to make direction to the life itself. It is because the purpose of prenatal life is only the preparation period for the earth life and its purpose is to create the foundation of the mind and the body. Whether the mother is smart enough to know this or is ignorant of this fact will have a great bearing on the personality formation history of her child. It makes a great difference on the inborn nature (the mental disposition of the soul and the personality of the mind) of the unborn child.

The dimension and mental disposition of consciousness, which is formed by the environment and experience of the personality formation history, makes a difference by whether it is Self-affirmation and Self-affection integrated by love, or Self-hatred and Self-denial dominated by resentment. The motivation of mind is directed according to the feelings of love or resentment and it will manifest and become phenomenon, whether good or bad, in all words and deeds, and health or illness.

1-31. All things are based on the principles of Self-determination and Self-responsibility

A person who connotes Self-denial and Self-hatred in themselves is always dominated by unpleasant feelings and complains about everything, even the weather. It doesn't matter what happens, they always complain, whether it`s raining or not, when it is hot or cold, sunny or cloudy. The problem is not in the weather or environment, but is because the person has unpleasant feelings dominated by hatred in his/her consciousness.

For instance, if you have only the mental disposition of Self-affirmation based on love, and never have feelings of anger inside, you will never be angry, and will accept everything as it is, without any doubt, unconditionally, even if you are slandered, abused, or beaten by others without any reason. Why? Because, since you have no feelings of anger inside yourself, it is impossible for you to be angry. On the other hand, what if you are filled with anger? Probably you will express your anger even though somebody only inadvertently touched your clothing. The reason for this kind of reaction is because your mind is filled with anger.

Chapter 1 ☆ The Starting Point

Even if people all over the world have compassion and mourn over you about your unhappiness, if you never feel any unhappiness, but instead, you are filled with happiness and gratitude every day, living cheerfully, are you unhappy? No, you are not unhappy. Whether you are happy or unhappy depends on your own consciousness and you are the only one who has the right to decide the direction of your own consciousness unreservedly, by your own free intention, according to the "rule of freedom" and the principle of Self-responsibility.

A person of character exercises the consciousness as a person of character, and an evil person exercises the consciousness as an evil person. All causes are directed and determined according to the "rule of the relative wave and relative original power" based on the spiritual dimension of the person. No matter how others criticize or evaluate you, those are irresponsible evaluations and you should not empathize or discharge negative feelings. You should bear Self-responsibility to Self-determination based on the "rule of freedom," and you should exercise Self-help to make efforts for Self-completion of the consciousness aiming to a higher level spiritual dimension. Whether you make yourself with gratitude and happiness, or complain with dissatisfaction, it is all based on the principle of Self-determination and Self-responsibility based on the "rule of freedom," and because of this, the entire universe exists in *the principle of equality*.

Therefore, whether you exercise your "soul mind" or "body mind," or act good or bad is determined by your own free intention. You have the absolute and unconditional right to perform all things based on the motivation, but so does everybody else. You and others are totally equal when you make Self-completion, by taking your own responsibility. In order to release Self-hatred, the root of all evil, it is important to establish Self-integration by drawing the separation boundary between you and others to make clear that whether your existence is the subject or the object, you are the cause or the result.

People who live the PARAREVO life recognize that they are the subject and the cause of all things happening to them by drawing the separation boundary between them and others, and are conscious of the importance of the PARAREVO concept to live their precious lives based on Self-responsibility. It is because this boundary will play an important role in completing Self-determination and Self-responsibility when you are at the big turning point of life.

You should recognize clearly, that the cause and subjectivity of your emotions toward all results are in yourself, so it is important to draw the separation boundary between oneself and others. Also, you should dispel the habit of mind to shift responsibility toward the outside, and do not fall into a feeling of being victimized by vicarious emotions. This is the best way to release Self-injurious behavior by Self-hatred, and you should direct the consciousness of Self-affection and Self-affirmation *by accepting everything as it is, unconditionally and entirely, with gratitude and happiness, toward yourself.*

People who live the "common way" construct the entire society based on the "principle of bad competition" by *the selfish lack of*

Chapter 1 ☆ The Starting Point

virtue and by the hypocrisy of Self-satisfaction with the mechanism of severe acquisition competition for evaluation by others, with the desire of the benefits in this world such as academic supremacy principles, economic supremacy principles and merit-based principles. They are considering it is good, without any doubt and putting it in the social system. Also they compete for winning or losing, measuring each other all the time, and exercise Self-inflicted activity, hurting their own soul by Self-hatred for the benefits in this world, which we will eventually lose.

People who live the way of PARAREVO consider the Self-affection that leads toward Self-Enlightenment and spiritual evolution in order to not lose their direction for completion in the spiritual world, as the first principle, by embracing as many people as possible with gratitude and happiness by *the virtue of unselfishness by Self-sacrifice*, based on the "principle of good competition." The virtue of unselfishness by Self-sacrifice is the way of PARAREVO life. It means that you sacrifice your physical world benefits such as status, reputation, and unnecessary property, open up the joyful emotional path of many people based on love, and give unconditional love to everyone and ask for nothing in return, and try to reach Self-Enlightenment and spiritual evolution, toward a higher spiritual dimension.

1-32. The rule of "exclusion theory by jealousy"

There is no doubt that experiences in prenatal and family environment are the most important factors in the personality formation history, and the biggest influence in the personality formation history is the emotional relationship based on the core of love with parents and ONSHU.

In particular, the spiritual dimension of the mother's personality and spirituality has a great influence on the children. Seeing the personality formation history of great saints and righteous people, they had very unusual backgrounds, and had great mothers, as the common factor. So, it could be said that the personality of the saints and the righteous, and their backbone of the spiritual consciousness entity that becomes the core of the individuality, had been formed in the womb by the *love of wise motherhood.* The emotional world of mother during pregnancy, and her personality dimension such as superiority or inferiority, will influence the fetus greatly.

I think that the emotional world and the personality dimension of Mary, the mother of Jesus, and Maya, the mother of Buddha, were extremely superior. So I could say that Jesus and Buddha had spent the ideal prenatal life with love. However, their actual life on earth was far from the ideal family life, because they were illegitimate, not biological children, they grew up in a poor and complex family environment.

The feeling of illegitimate children who have been raised by the biological father but different mother, or biological mother but different father, might have a strong envy and/or jealousy by differentiation of love, and being conscious of others eyes and others evaluation about everything. They are easily dominated by earth logical and secular values such as appearances, vanity, status, honor, and property, and they may tend to be tormented by paranoia, despair, and/or suspicion.

The most unpleasant emotion that we should distinguish carefully in our life is our inner *mind of jealousy* derived from *the deficiency syndrome of love*. The jealous mind makes you fall victim to Self-hatred and Self-denial, and invites Self-destruction by Self-injurious behavior. I call this state of mind the *"rule of Self-destruction,"* derived from the *"rule of exclusion theory by jealousy."* This rule can be explained like this. If we have a jealous mind and push away the ones we are jealous of, by exercising the consciousness exclusively with the motivation to exclude them, it results in losing our own place and losing the ones we love as well. Finally, we will invite Self-destruction by Self-injurious behavior, such as cancer, depression, and/or suicide.

This rule also manifests various roots of evils. For example, there would be discord between a daughter-in-law and father-in-law, and daughter-in-law and mother-in-law. If mother-in-law falls into the illusion that her beloved son was stolen by her daughter-in-law, then she treats her cruelly and tries to expel her, it could happen that the mother-in-law would lose her precious and irreplaceable son by accident or illness and/or she herself might be struck down by an unexpected incurable disease or strange disease and would eventually destroy herself. This "rule of exclusion theory by jealousy" has brought on various conflicts, corruptions and discriminations which occur anytime and anywhere, not only in the family, but in companies and society, also.

The popular Japanese novelists, Ryunosuke Akutagawa and Osamu Dazai, and the Nobel Prize winner, Yasunari Kawabata, are examples of the typical type of people who pushed themselves to the limit by Self-hatred and rejected the existence of themselves from this world and committed Self-injurious behavior, suicide. This was caused by the "rule of exclusion theory by jealousy." When you look at their personality formation history, you will find a closed and very negative factor of their mind which was because they could not dispel ONSHU from their background. They had sad and miserable backgrounds and potentially had a common consciousness of Self-hatred and Self-denial caused by the lacking of parental love syndrome. They were adopted or illegitimate children who could not receive love from their birth parents, and their growing up environments were extremely harsh. Their novels were written by those feelings. They wrote down the conflicts between the world of their ideal love and the world of ONSHU in their novels as if they wanted to erase their feelings of hatred and denial. They saw the widely different gap in ideal and reality, between the ideal of love in the virtual world in their novels, and themselves who were filled with hatred and aversion in the real world where they had to live. As a result, there was an increasing conflict and fluctuation between their "soul mind" and "body mind," so that they could not compensate the mind of sorrow and grudge. Thus, they committed suicide, which was Self-destruction as a result of choice of struggle and agony, suffering from the opposite feelings of hatred and denial in their own evaluation even though one of them received the Nobel Prize as the global evaluation. They had feelings of jealousy toward the virtual world of love and ideal which they created in their novels. So, by the "rule of exclusion theory by jealousy," they excluded their own existence from this world by their own hands by Self-injurious behavior, because of their feelings of hatred toward themselves in reality.

The "rule of exclusion theory by jealousy" is the root of all evil in the unfortunate history of human beings. Even now, it still exists in the core of the negative spiral of religious struggle and ethnic strife, and follows the unbroken chain of misery.

1-33. End of material civilization

We have obtained many conveniences and material richness by the benefit of the scientific civilization, and an insatiable achievement in evolution and progress such as the shortening of distance and time and securing vast energies. However, ironically, we cannot deny the fact that most of those scientific civilizations have achieved evolution and progress together with wars and the development of weapons, which are the symbol of violence.

The best examples are the development of nuclear power and internet technology in the IT revolution. They were born from the military industries. And when we human beings developed the atomic bomb, the mass slaughter weapons, it could be said that we opened Pandora's box, the door to Self-destruction. During the 1970's, the Cold War era, with the number of atomic bombs possessed by the U.S. and the Soviet Union, it was possible to destroy the earth itself, a dozen times over.

The 20th century was the era of conflict in ideology between capitalism and communism, and fortunately we were able to avoid serious tragedy because of the collapse of the Soviet Union.

However, in the 21st century, a new threat occurred in the first year of the century. On September 11, 2001, the Islamic fundamentalist terrorist group attacked the World Trade Center in the U.S., and simultaneously executed multiple acts of terrorism. That was another type of violent destructive act.

In the 21st century, the world economy will reach chaos under the collapse of the capitalistic economy, and the situation of the world will expose itself to the threat of nuclear terrorism with victim consciousness and shifting of responsibility by fanatical believers in monotheism.

The ideology of communism is materialism based on the theoretical framework and values in this world, so it does not reach the paradigm beyond the verge of life and death. However, since religions theorize the paradigm Self-righteously, beyond the verge of life and death, human beings will face the most dangerous new threat. When extremist fanatics such as the Jewish fundamentalists and Islamic fundamentalists obtain atomic bombs, all human beings will be exposed to an extremely volatile crisis.

We might have already reached the critical time, so we should transcend the theoretical framework and values of existing religions and promote the consciousness revolution by the emergence of a new paradigm as soon as possible, and suggest the direction that human beings must take.

1-34. The 21st century is the era of consciousness revolution

Since we understand that the existing purpose and value in life are preparation for the spiritual life, and there is no other meaning, we have to face our life seriously and distinguish between the necessary things and the unnecessary things in preparation for going to the spiritual world. In order to do so, we have to comprehend the mechanism and system of the spiritual world, verify it, and understand clearly what we should prepare and should not prepare for in this world. To accomplish this, we should verify things existing in the spiritual world and things not existing in the spiritual world, distinguishing between necessary things and unnecessary things, clarifying the purpose and values for the benefits in this world and the benefits in the spiritual world and lead our life in the right direction.

In the spiritual world, there is no physical body or concept of time, so cause and effect immediately respond and become phenomenon. No one in the spiritual world but oneself will be a cause, and everything manifested becomes the phenomenon, based on the cause of the spiritual dimension of one's spiritual consciousness entity, so that one who has a beautiful spiritual consciousness entity in the higher spiritual dimension will always manifest as the phenomenon of the beautiful world.

Whether in the spiritual world or in this world, for those with a spiritual consciousness entity filled with dissatisfaction and complaints in the lower spiritual dimension, the world of dissatisfaction and complaints will always be manifested and become the phenomenon, and for those with a spiritual consciousness entity full of gratitude and happiness, the world of gratitude and happiness is manifested and becomes the phenomenon.

Also, the position in the spiritual world is determined by the relativity of the feeling at the moment of death, based on the principle of Self-responsibility. If your soul has completed Self-enlightenment and spiritual evolution, it means you can completely accept everything unconditionally, with gratitude and happiness as it is in any situation. If you have an accident or get an illness and die as a result, you accept it with gratitude and do not fall victim to negative emotions, so you can be relative and go to a beautiful spiritual world in a higher dimension.

Contents for Book 2 : Chapter Two☆The Deriving point

2-1. The existence purpose of consciousness and existence value of individuality

2-2. Formation process of consciousness based on the personality formation history

2-3. Formation processes of consciousness and the three elements

2-4. Verifying the "Cluster" of spiritual consciousness entity

2-5. Original existence consciousnesses are the primordial consciousness of terrestrial life

2-6. Formation processes of "original existence consciousnesses" and the two elements

2-7. Transitions of "instinctive survival consciousnesses" in history

2-8. The terrestrial life has common desire consciousness and performs common ecological action

2-9. Spiritual evolution is the release from "instinctive survival consciousnesses"

2-10. Sexual maturity and spiritual evolution

2-11. Release of undifferentiated sexual desire consciousness and spirituality evolution

2-12. Subconscious is derived from the physical and spiritual formation history

2-13. "Reincarnation consciousness" is the direct subconscious

2-14. "Genetic consciousness" is the indirect subconscious

2-15. The fundamental difference between subconscious of the soul and the body

2-16. Law of causality in Buddhism theory is untruth

2-17. Genetic linkage and reincarnation are both related to the principle of Self-responsibility

2-18. Emerging consciousnesses are formed in two stages

2-19. The purpose of the personality formation and the physical body formationin the prenatal life

2-20. Ideal personality formation in the prenatal life

2-21. Taboos of personality formations in the womb

2-22. Ideal physical formation in the prenatal life

2-23. Taboos of physical formation in the prenatal life

2-24. Womb is a sanctuary for "change by birth and re-birth"

2-25. Womb is a sanctuary for physical evolution

2-26. Womb is a sanctuary of spiritual evolution

2-27. Personality formation based on the earth environment

2-28. The existing purpose and the existing value in the earth life

2-29. Earth life determines the spiritual dimension
2-30. Ideal personality formation in the earth life
2-31. Emotional relationship between child and parents, and the "rule of relativity"
2-32. The ideal family of love, which cannot be built with religion or philosophy
2-33. Emerging consciousnesses and the importance of maternal love
2-34. Emerging consciousnesses is the final chapter of consciousness formation
2-35. Time axis domination by the brain memory
2-36. Human history is a journey of self-discovery
2-37. Acquisition competition for the evaluation by others and integration disorder
2-38. The existence of SHINSEI, which is the root consciousness
2-39. True inherent nature existing in the root consciousness
2-40. Limits of the material world on the time axis
2-41. The basic principle of the Universe
2-42. Relative subject and the "principles of dimensional integration"
2-43. Relative object and the "principle of dimensional domination"
2-44. The "rule of the relative original power" based on the "rule of balance"
2-45. Life creation process on the earth star
2-46. The earth star is a unique planet
2-47. Mathematical evaluation leads to competition and domination
2-48. Words and languages are specific presence on the earth star
2-49. The earth star performs the role and responsibilities of a prison planet
2-50. The "rule of give and take" on the earth star
2-51. The "rule of give and give" of the universe
2-52. Prison in the prison star (earth) is a geriatric hospital
2-53. The degree of freedom of consciousness and the degree of acceptance of love based on spiritual dimension
2-54. Energy wave level in the spiritual dimension
2-55. Earth logic is legalized by the principle of domination
2-56. Environmental adaptation is a driving force for evolution
2-57. Wisdom and desire is a bipolar structure of the brain
2-58. Science civilizations lead spiritual culture
2-59. The universe is penetrated by the principle of integration
2-60. Now is the era when the Christian Bible, Buddhist writings, and other scriptures begin to fade

2-61. The earth star is filled with delusions and illusions by supposition and speculation
2-62. Religion will become archaic and fade away
2-63. Sexual desires cannot be released by religion
2-64. The 21st century plunges into the era of ending the prison star
2-65. The crisis can be avoided by liberation from religious curse
2-66. Religious struggles are the common crisis of the earth star
2-67. The Old Testament is the genealogy of genetic linkage from Eve
2-68. The core of ONSHU of Judaism and Islam
2-69. The triangle relationship of sorrow and ONSHU that happened in Abraham's family
2-70. Great virtues of unselfishness by Self-sacrifice
2-71. Analysis of personality formation history of Adolf Hitler
2-72. The "rule of sorrow and ONSYU in the triangle relationship" in Jacob's family
2-73. Trial and persecution produce spiritual evolution and prosperity
2-74. Love and ONSHU are inherited by sentiments of women
2-75. Love pillage by King David and ONSHU of Uriah
2-76. Analysis of the personality formation history of Jesus Christ
2-77. Historical lessons in the Bible

For more information please contact us :
Self-Healing Study and Practice Group
(info@selfhealing.co.in)

www.ingramcontent.com/pod-product-compliance
Lightning Source LLC
Chambersburg PA
CBHW070248100426
42743CB00011B/2182